They have helped make Asheville a culinary destination in the heart of the South. When they were opening Cúrate, Katie reached out to me for insight, and so the next day I flew to Asheville with four of my top chefs. My team and I, we wanted to be there, not only to lend a hand but also to be part of what was happening. Katie and Félix share a dream of mine—to bring American restaurants with a Spanish spirit not only to major cities but deeper into the U.S. Katie and Félix were living out this dream, and I just had to be there. The same way they were next to me years before.

As a Spanish chef in America, I am so jealous of this book. Nobody embraces Spain in the heart of America with more poetry, passion, and perfection than Katie. She and her husband, Félix, are family to me, and I feel great joy seeing how she has grown as a person and as a chef.

**–JOSÉ ANDRÉS**
*Chef/Owner, ThinkFoodGroup and minibar by José Andrés*

# CÚRATE

# CÚRATE

Authentic Spanish Food FROM an American Kitchen

KATIE BUTTON

WITH Genevieve Ko

PHOTOGRAPHY BY Evan Sung

FLATIRON
BOOKS
NEW YORK

www.flatironbooks.com

COVER AND BOOK DESIGN BY SHUBHANI SARKAR

PHOTOGRAPHS BY EVAN SUNG

The Library of Congress Cataloging-in-
Publication Data is available upon request.

ISBN 978-1-250-05944-4 (paper-over-board)
ISBN 978-1-250-05945-1 (e-book)

Our books may be purchased in bulk for pro-
motional, educational, or business use. Please
contact your local bookseller or the Macmillan
Corporate and Premium Sales Department at
1-800-221-7945, extension 5442, or by e-mail at
MacmillanSpecialMarkets@macmillan.com.

First Edition: October 2016

10 9 8 7 6 5 4 3 2 1

FOR GISELA

# CONTENTS

## ie nada...
## ¿una copita?

sherry wines or wine by the glass...
...check our wine list

white, extra dry, or gran reserva red $7

...r white $9

...quiles- red $9

...f sparkling cava or red wine, made
...panaché, a blend of estrella da...
...n... we dare you not to spill...
...reau, & flamed orange pe...
...tanqueray, perucchi re...
...d fresh lemon...simp...
...know a good gi...
...ndricks gin &...
...spain, ma...
...ier &...
...ou...

...ghland
...ger $4.
...50

...bottled beer and c...
...ger (GF) $5, inedi...

...ian ale $9 or **negra stout**...

...r from asturias, glass $9, bott...

...by the bottle or glass
...on or bitter lemon or tonic $3

...ea $2.50

## embutidos y quesos
### charcuterie & chees...
featuring fermin brand cured meats

**jamón serrano fermín** $8 (LF, NF)
delicious dry cured spanish ham (GF: No Br...

**jamón ibérico fermín** $11 (LF, NF)
cured ham from the famous black-footed
ibérico pigs of spain (GF: No Bread)

**jamón ibérico de bellota 5J** $20 (LF, NF)
100% pure ibérico pigs, acorn fattened and
free range, giving it a unique and
exceptionally nutty flavor (GF: No Bread)

**tabla de jamón** $18 (LF, NF)
a selection of all three cured hams, a great
way to compare their subtleties (GF: No Bread)

**tabla de embutidos ibéricos** $15 (NF)
explore the tradition of the finest spanish charcuterie
w/ ibérico de bellota: lomo...

nuestros vi...
pa... a empez...
espa... sparkl...
N/V... R...
... R...
... nve...
201...
N/V...
200...

BOT/COPA
$28 / $7
$48 / $12
$80
$100

---

## frit

**croq**
trad

**\*pata**
cris
a s

**bere**
frie
hon

**chis**
spi...
the

## bocadi
*sandwi...*

**\*bocadill**
roasted
olive spr
bonito tu

**\*bocadill**
catalan...
...ramel...

...

...
pic...

**\*espárra**
white aspa...
vinaigrette &
"light as air" m...

## ensalada de toma
kumato tomato salad...
bonito tuna, black olives,
olive oil & reserve sherry v...

# FOREWORD

## FERRAN ADRIÀ

I TYPICALLY CAN REMEMBER EACH AND EVERY person who has worked at elBulli, both in the kitchen and the dining room. But some I recall with special affection—for their professionalism and their character, but also for their enthusiasm, their utmost involvement, their passion for work, and their respect for other colleagues and for the industry. There is no doubt that Katie Button and Félix Meana belong in this very small group.

Their story is worthy of elBulli. It is known that the journey to our restaurant in Cala Montjoi was full of random chances, of coincidences, of risks for taking the road less traveled. I believe that this is also their case. I met Félix, a *rosinc* [native of Roses] from head to toe, when he had already achieved a good career in the world of hospitality. He quickly proved to have pure elBulli DNA, which does not often happen. Indeed, to fit into our restaurant, it wasn't enough to be very good; you also had to have something special.

And this guy who arrived in 2004 had it. Until 2008, Félix worked closely with the dining room directors, lending the necessary support and proving to be one of the pillars of service. During the winter, elBulli's off-season, Félix continued his front-of-house training, primarily in the United States. At Minibar and Café Atlántico, one of the restaurants of my friend José Andrés, he met Katie, a chemical engineer who was working there at the same time.

Starting then, their respective life plans were united. Professionally, both still had to go through a few stages before launching their own projects. Katie worked in the elBulli dining room in 2008, after which she worked for the first time in a professional kitchen in the pastry department of Jean-Georges in New York. She also worked the garde manger station with José Andrés at The Bazaar in Los Angeles.

In 2009, Katie felt ready to join the pastry team at elBulli, which was run by Mateu Casañas under the supervision of Albert Adrià. There, we saw that she was a person who learned at breakneck speed, thanks to her meticulous nature, her great capacity for concentration, and her rapid understanding of the Spanish language and culinary processes. I can easily say that I do not know many people as gifted as Katie in the kitchen.

In 2011, I learned that the project Katie and Félix planned to undertake together was their first restaurant. Cúrate, situated in the city of Asheville, North Carolina, features a great gastronomic formula based on quality Spanish tapas. Contrary to what you might think,

Asheville is in a privileged circuit of cities that, while perhaps not well known, are places where things happen, where things are created, where businesses open. Asheville is a city with amazing gastronomic offerings, to which were then added Katie and Félix. Brilliant!

Three years later, they went one step further and dared to open a second restaurant, Nightbell. It's a restaurant format that's difficult to classify but is enormously attractive. And today comes this book, a success whichever way you look at it. Tapas from Cúrate are adapted to be larger dishes for meals at home; these are joined with other recipes that translate Katie's experiences in Roses, Catalonia, and that will, without a doubt, be a perfect introduction to Spanish cuisine in American homes.

Enjoy, then, this book by the hand of Katie Button. Stroll through our rich Spanish cuisine, adapted by a cook who has managed to fully capture its essence and make it hers, and who, with Félix Meana, has created a perfect combination that rarely occurs in the world of hospitality. I have no doubt: This will be just the first editorial fruit from my two Asheville friends.

CÚRATE

# INTRODUCTION

IN MY HOME, PEOPLE ARE ALWAYS EATING—whether it's a freshly made pan con tomate thrown together from the last of the ripe summer tomatoes, good olive oil, and some crusty bread; a big pan of seafood paella shared amongst three generations in a backyard summer feast; or a lunch of leftover tortilla española alongside a simple green salad scattered with candied nuts. No matter the meal, cooking and serving delicious Spanish food at home is much easier than you might think. When you envision Spanish food, you may think tapas—small dishes meant to be served with drinks. And while flavorful bites like banderillas and empanadas provide plenty of inspirations for entertaining, tapas are just a slice of what Spanish cuisine has to offer.

The Spanish cuisine of today in many ways reflects the privations of their civil war years, when home cooks had to be creative with humble ingredients. As a result, simple, comforting food that highlights the beautiful produce, seafood, and meat grown, caught, and raised all around the country forms the basis of Spanish cuisine. Given the fertility of the land and huge coastal areas, Spanish food has always been about the ingredients. And then there are the flavors. Unlike most other countries in Western Europe, Spain is heavily influenced by the spices and seasonings of North Africa. Regional cuisines within Spain vary not only geographically but culturally as well. Galicia, the Basque Country, and Catalonia have their own languages and almost feel like countries within the country. However different their heritages may be, regions within Spain share a philosophy of cooking and dining that places food at the center of familial and unpretentious everyday celebrations.

The food itself is as comforting as the ritual of sharing it. Cúrate, a Spanish restaurant in Asheville, North Carolina, that I opened in 2011 along with my husband, Félix, and my parents, Liz and Ted, translates to "cure yourself," an imperative I take to heart when welcoming guests for a meal. The traditional Spanish cuisine we serve honors the seasonal, local ingredients of the Blue Ridge Mountains and celebrates Southern simplicity and hospitality while championing authentic Spanish dishes and techniques. If these sound like contradictions, they're no more surprising than a former chemical and biomolecular engineering major at Cornell University dropping out of a PhD program to pursue a culinary career. But first, let me tell you how I got to that point.

## MY STORY

Growing up in Greenville, South Carolina, I developed an abiding love of pulled pork with mustard sauce, smoked ribs and chicken, boiled peanuts, and the healing power of soul food. Back home, my grandma and mom slowly stewed collard greens and baked tomato pies and peach pies. For my birthday every year, they followed an orange sponge cake recipe from the *Heritage Southern Food Cookbook* that came out of the pan as light and airy as a cloud.

When my mom launched her own catering company, my palate continued to expand beyond Southern cuisine. Our home kitchen always buzzed with activity, and commercial freezers

lined our basement walls. The scent of Mom's wonderful rosemary butter rolls hung in the air until the smoke from seared beef tenderloin took over. Any leftovers from catering jobs ended up as my brown-bag lunches. One day it'd be baked brie with raspberries and mushroom paté; on other days I'd get spinach wrapped in phyllo or white bean shrimp salad with goat cheese. If Mom had dough scraps after forming tiny tart shells, she'd fill them with jam and sprinkle them with sugar to bake into lunchbox treats.

I discovered a wide range of flavors early on, and even more important, I quickly learned the joy of feeding others. By the time I was twelve, I was the one making the birthday cakes for our family: German chocolate for Mom and Boston cream pie for Dad.

But as much as I loved food, I never dreamt of cooking professionally. Always strong in math and science, I majored in chemical and biomolecular engineering at Cornell University and then went to Paris for my master's degree. I lived in an apartment in the fifth arrondissement, right on the rue Mouffetard. Dining out didn't work with my student stipend, but examining all

the food stands on my street was free. Each little store had a specialty: brioche here, fish there, pork at this butcher, rabbit at the other. I'd smell and feel every fruit and vegetable and, when I could afford it, I'd splurge on some. I spent what little money I had on the few ingredients I could afford and *Le meilleur de la cuisine française saveurs et terroirs*, a huge tome that covered every classic French preparation and plating. Learning to make quiche and poisson en croute in an apartment with no kitchen counters, I bleached a three-square-foot section of floor, taped it off as my work surface so no one would walk on it, and rolled and folded dough over and over again to perfect the pastry.

When I returned to the U.S., I enrolled in a PhD program to continue my graduate studies. But as I continued to cook at home, I couldn't shake the feeling that my heart belonged in the kitchen. I decided to drop out of the PhD program. Living in Washington, D.C., at the time, I walked into one of star chef José Andrés's Spanish restaurants to apply for a job as a server. I went on to work in his kitchens and, from there, I had the privilege of doing a seven-month stage in elBulli's pastry kitchen. Revolutionary chef Ferran Adrià's restaurant in Roses, Spain (now closed), was the very best in the world at that time. My stint cooking there was even chronicled by Lisa Abend in her book *The Sorcerer's Apprentices*.

The experience was intense, to put it mildly. During our first week, the whole staff had to polish all of the rocks in the restaurant's garden entrance and replace them in their exact positions. Doing so taught us the attention to detail we needed in order to succeed in creating a restaurant experience as impeccable as the one elBulli promised. Each day, I put my head down and did every task asked of me as flawlessly as I possibly could, as fast as I could. As the end of my time there neared, I was tempted to stay and pursue a full-time position.

But there was another commitment I needed to honor—this time to my parents. They had founded the Heirloom Hospitality Group and chosen Asheville, North Carolina, as the location for its first restaurant. When they generously

invited my husband, Félix, whom I'd met while working for José Andrés, and me to be their partners, we were thrilled to accept.

Given Félix's Spanish heritage and my experience cooking Spanish cuisine, we decided to open a tapas restaurant with my parents. It's a true family business. Mom's the CEO and she keeps the whole company running, handling everything from human resources and payroll to public and media relations. Félix has decades of experience running the front-of-the-house and continues to do so at Cúrate, along with overseeing the entire beverage program. Dad takes care of all the finances, keeping us afloat in so many ways.

## CÚRATE

In this cookbook, I've taken the best principles of Spanish cooking and shown how to apply them in an American kitchen. For example, many people in Spain tend to shop more frequently throughout the week, going to their local markets daily for produce, meats, and seafood. I've

made sure that the recipes in this book allow you to do your shopping for the week all at once, as we tend to do in the U.S. But of course I encourage you to shop the way the Spaniards do whenever possible, in order to serve your friends and family a large variety of the freshest ingredients. Unlike in the U.S., in Spain the main meal of the day is generally cooked for a leisurely lunch, and then dinner is a quick salad. In this book, I've placed recipes in categories more in line with the American conception of lighter, quick-prep lunches and hearty dinners. When I create dishes for the Cúrate menu, I always start by thinking about the main ingredient and how to make it shine. Using authentic Spanish techniques, I expand upon classic Spanish recipes, infusing them along the way with the culinary traditions of the South. If I'm making canelones, I can swap out the meat stuffing for anything, but I've got to have the pasta rolled, smothered in béchamel and cheese, and broiled. For white asparagus with mayonnaise, I aerate my sauce to make it fluffier and top it all with torn tarragon leaves. You won't find the herbs in any classic recipe, but they brighten the dish with a scent I love without compromising the essence of the original. I never veer so far from tradition that a dish loses its soul.

One of my greatest struggles when opening Cúrate was figuring out how to replicate the home cooking of Spain for hundreds of diners a day. Learning to cook in Spain is a lifelong journey, with recipes often passed down from generation to generation. Typically, friends and family will whip together similar dishes without a recipe, purely working from the memory of cooking those dishes time and again with mothers and grandmothers at home. I've worked hard to make these authentic Spanish dishes approachable and replicable so that anyone, regardless of their heritage (and regardless of whether or not they come from a long line of great cooks) can prepare them. In all my years of scientific research, the goal of each experiment was to perform the same test again and again to see how results differed. I approached my restaurant dishes the same way, while implementing the kitchen organization and culinary precision that I learned at elBulli. I create and test my recipes and weigh ingredients to the gram; I take temperatures of everything from hot oil to the center of a roast to bubbling caramel; I time confits and measure the diameter of cookies. And then, I let it all go and share a delicious meal with friends and family. And you can, too. When you're cooking at home, don't worry if things don't go quite right. Follow the recipe, follow your instincts, and enjoy the process—and most of all, the food.

Even though the food and drinks in this cookbook will make you feel as if you're sharing in the dining experience we're so proud of at Cúrate, they've been adapted (and in some cases even improved) for home kitchens. I've kept the flavors and textures and included the smart techniques I've learned over the years, but found substitutes for things like siphons, immersion circulators, and deep fryers in recipes like the Ensalada de Alcachofas (page 53) and the Espárragos Blancos con Mayonesa (page 147). If anything, the book's recipes will taste even more like they came straight out of a Spanish home kitchen, which is what we strive for at the restaurant. Most Spanish dishes taste best when made at home.

The hardest part of Spanish cooking is changing your mind-set about meal preparation. It's not about speed; it's about convenience, ease, and, above all, pleasure. Félix's mom never frantically whipped up dinner in 20 minutes (though the tuna tomato salad takes less than 10). Instead, like moms all over the country, she leisurely cooked classics—tortilla española, canelones, albóndigas—when she wasn't pressed for time. Many dishes not only hold up well but also are meant to be made ahead and eaten at room temperature.

When entertaining, I love to spend time with my guests once they arrive. It's so much nicer to have things done and be able to share a glass of wine with friends. Maybe I'll have made the brandada the night before, or the beer-braised chicken. In fact, any braise works well made ahead and then reheated for company. In the

summer, I'll have spice-rubbed and marinated meats ready to toss on the grill. Imagine the thrill you feel when you've baked a coffee cake and the next morning you see it there on the counter, just waiting for you to cut another slice. That's the happiness most Spanish recipes give the cook.

At the heart of Cúrate and of this book is honest Spanish food and the dining culture that surrounds it. At the restaurant, we offer a tapas experience, sending out small plates through-out the meal for the whole table to share. If you want to prepare a dozen or more recipes from this book for a tapas party, you'll have fun doing it. But most of the dishes ahead are meant to be eaten on their own or with one other dish or just some good bread. When you go through these pages, pick a recipe or two based on your mealtime scenario. Doing a dinner party? Braise oxtail a few days ahead and simmer again right before your guests arrive. Last-minute cock-tails? Throw together some banderillas. Week-

night date night? Wrap a trout in Ibérico ham, pan-fry it fast, and eat the whole fish together off a shared plate. Busy kids' schedules? Make croquetas on the weekend and fry them straight from the fridge all week long. Your kids will never tire of them and will love you forever.

In this book, I re-create the meals I have at home with Félix and our daughter, Gisela, and the ones we share when visiting Félix's family on the Costa Brava. There, his mother, brothers, aunts, and uncles make big family-style platters and casseroles and set them all down at the same time. We gather around the table, doling servings out to the kids and each other and laugh and eat and eat and eat. We hope you'll experience the same pleasure of a leisurely Spanish meal on this side of the Atlantic.

### TE QUIERO MUCHO COMO LA TRUCHA AL TRUCHO.

That Spanish saying literally translates to "I love you like a female trout loves a male trout." It's just

a silly way of expressing how much you care for someone, but it means a lot to me. When Félix and I got married, we decided to engrave the phrase on our wedding bands. His is inscribed with "te quiero mucho" and mine with the ending.

We met working together and that's been really important in our lives. My progression as a chef is totally dependent on the fact that I met Félix when I did, and the success of Cúrate stems entirely from our unity as a team. We complement each other perfectly. I handle the food and he oversees the beverages and service. But our roles are much more fluid than that, and there are a million and one ways in which we're compatible. We're rarely apart for more than a few hours and while our debates over business decisions (or our baby's sleep schedule) can get heated, we resolve any tension really quickly. There isn't a place where our professional lives end and our marriage begins because our relationship started in the business. We always say we never would be who we are without each other.

Félix claims he knew the moment he saw me that I was the one. On our first date, we hit it off right away. We both love food, so that was a big connection for us, but we immediately fell into such a natural rapport. I had never felt quite so loved quite so easily and readily.

As our relationship grew, our careers evolved together, too. Félix, who knew I wanted to continue pursuing a career in restaurants, convinced me to let him ask Ferran and Albert Adrià, whom he worked for in Roses, if I could work at elBulli. Félix arranged for me to work half a season at elBulli as a server, and the experience blew my mind. I knew then that this was the life I wanted.

I was offered the opportunity to return to elBulli, this time as a cook in the pastry kitchen, for a full season. During that stretch, Félix and I made two of our biggest life decisions. We got engaged and partnered with my parents to open a Spanish restaurant in Asheville.

The rest, as they say, is history.

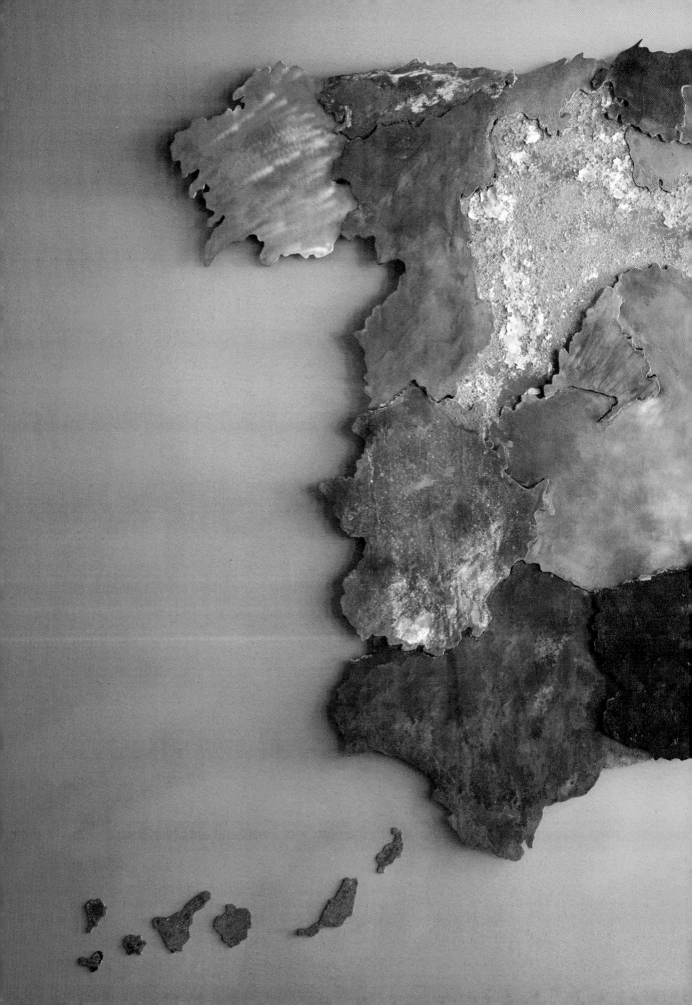

ONE THING I LOVE ABOUT SPANISH FOOD IS ITS regionality. There are so many different areas with so many specific cuisines, and I've just begun to scratch the surface. In San Sebastian bars, they serve pintxos (little skewers) with sidra (cider) on tap. In Segovia, you get suckling pig. In the Canary Islands, potatoes come in all forms. In Madrid, you can spend hours savoring cocido Madrileño, a multicourse stew of meat, beans, and vegetables. In Rioja, the suckling lamb is unbelievable. Even though each region's cuisine is distinct, the dishes of many regions can be served together and still taste wonderful.

# PANTRY

ONE OF THE GREAT THINGS ABOUT COOKING SPAN-ish cuisine is how easy it is to find the ingredients you need. Even if you can't track down an item in your local store, you can easily order it online. Below are some staples.

## ESSENTIALS

**Blended Oil:** In Spain, olive oil comes in a variety of grades for different uses. The closest approximation to the mild Spanish olive oil reserved for cooking is a 50/50 blend of canola and olive oil. The Spectrum brand is available at Whole Foods and other supermarkets, but you can make your own mix with half canola and half olive oil that's mild in flavor, such as Arbequina.

**Olive Oil:** I keep a bottle of extra-virgin for cooking and a higher-quality extra-virgin Arbequina for dressing salads and making sauces.

**Canola Oil:** For high-heat frying and searing, I sometimes use this oil.

**Kosher Salt:** Proper seasoning is crucial to great flavor, so I measured the exact amounts of salt in nearly all of my recipes. I use Diamond Crystal Kosher Salt—here, the brand does matter. Both Morton and David's kosher salt have larger crystals, which taste saltier. If that's all you can find, scale down my amounts by about 25%. Even if you are using Diamond Crystal Kosher, you should taste your dishes again before serving and add more salt if you'd like. Taste the food at the temperature you want to eat it, then season to taste.

**Black Pepper:** I don't give measured amounts for black pepper because I prefer grinding right onto whatever I'm seasoning. An even sprinkle is all you need.

**Pimentón:** Smoked Spanish paprika comes sweet, hot, or bittersweet. I keep only the first two on hand. The most aromatic and well-balanced pimentón is labeled de la Vera for its region of origin.

**Dry Wine:** For white wine, a solid Albariño is inexpensive and worth keeping on hand. For red, choose a budget-friendly dry wine that you'd be happy sipping, too. I use wine often in my recipes and anything not cooked can be drunk.

**Sherry:** For cooking, there's no need to splurge on the stuff you'd drink. Any dry cooking sherry will do, such as the Gibson and Taylor brands.

**Sherry Vinegar:** Any sherry vinegar is fine for cooking. For dressing salads or drizzling, look for small bottles of aged reserved vinegar. I have a bottle of vinegar that's been aged for 50 years, and I love it. It's complex, intense, and will last a while if used sparingly.

**Saffron:** These threads are pricey—but incomparable in taste. Get tiny boxes. My recipes rarely call for more than a pinch.

**Bay Leaves:** If you see fresh ones in your store's produce section, pick up a pack. Any leaves you don't use will naturally dry in your fridge (or on your counter). Don't dump them! Just keep them

in an airtight container and use them. There's no need to then buy dried bay leaves; you've just made your own. If you can find only dried bay leaves, they work just as well even if they don't taste quite as fresh.

Spanish Canned Goods

**Piquillo Peppers:** These conical red peppers are sweeter and have thinner walls than standard red bell peppers. The best ones are from Spain and roasted over wood fire before being peeled and packed. If you buy cans and don't finish them all at once, transfer the peppers to another airtight container and refrigerate until you need them again.

**Tuna Packed in Olive Oil:** If you think you don't like tuna, you need to try the varieties from Spain. Bonito is the preferred fish; it's smaller, milder, and moister than others. Look for the

large fillets packed in cans or glass jars. Ortiz is a good brand and the one we stock at Cúrate.

**Anchovies:** I use the fillets packed in olive oil, not the salted ones. Ortiz sells some of the best anchovies I've ever had, specifically their la gran anchoa.

**Boquerónes:** These anchovies are not technically canned; they're sold in the refrigerated section. They're fresh fillets that have been marinated, almost cured really, in a mixture of vinegar and olive oil and sometimes herbs and spices. Again, Ortiz is the brand that's both most widely available and consistently delicious.

**White Asparagus:** The best juicy, sweet spears with nearly floral notes are grown and packaged in Navarra. Look for the denomination of origin (D.O.) label on the jars or cans before buying.

# GEAR

I DON'T USE ANY SPECIALTY TOOLS WHEN COOKING with the exception of paella pans and a food mill for mashed potatoes. You probably already have everything below, but if not, stop by a store to pick up whatever you're missing to be able to cook everything from this book.

**Cast-Iron Skillet:** The one pan I turn to most is my well-seasoned 14-inch cast-iron skillet passed down to me from my grandmother. Get one big cast-iron skillet, season it well, and keep it seasoned. Cast-iron heats the most evenly and lasts for generations.

**Heavy Skillets:** Keep at least one large, heavy skillet, either copper or aluminum-clad, on hand for searing.

**Nonstick Skillet:** The only surefire way to flip a tortilla (page 25) is by using a nonstick skillet.

**Dutch Oven:** Get at least one large, deep enameled cast-iron Dutch oven with a lid for braises and stews.

**Stockpots and Saucepans:** You'll need large ones with lids for soups and stews and for boiling ingredients from potatoes to octopus.

**Paella Pan:** If you're committed to making paella, invest in a good paella pan and season it well. I like the ones from Pata Negra.

**Half-Sheet Pans:** Buy heavy commercial ones. They'll last you a long time and can be used for everything from baking cakes to roasting vegetables to holding ingredients.

**Bakeware:** If you plan on trying my desserts (pages 231 to 257), you'll need a variety of baking dishes, as well as an ice cream maker.

**Food Processor:** I use a large Cuisinart for occasional chopping and slicing, as well as for making mayonnaise (page 147) and allioli (page 182).

**Blender:** I prefer the power of a Vitamix blender. You can buy a blender in department stores, big box stores, and other kitchenware stores. It creates the creamiest and smoothest soups.

**Sharp Knives:** I rely on a chef's knife most often, but I use a paring knife for smaller vegetables sometimes. A bread knife comes in handy anytime you need to slice a loaf.

**Peeler:** This is essential for most vegetables, and is ideal for preparing strips of citrus peels for cocktails.

**Microplane Zester:** I keep mine handy for zesting citrus.

**Box Grater:** The large holes work well for grating tomatoes, and the smaller holes for hard cheeses.

Can Opener: Some of Spain's greatest ingredients come in cans. Be ready to open them.

Silicone Spatulas: I use the flat ones for scraping bowls clean and the offset one for removing fried eggs from pans.

Wooden Spoons: These are my go-to stirrers for the stovetop.

Measuring Cups, Spoons, and a Kitchen Scale: Precision is key to nailing any of these recipes. While you should season dishes to taste, start by making them exactly as written, measuring according to the specifications in the ingredient list.

## JUST A LITTLE NOTE ON FOOD SAFETY

At my restaurant, I uphold the highest health standards for everything coming out of my kitchen. Any time I'm handling raw chicken or other meat, I wash my hands repeatedly and vigorously sanitize every surface around me. But I always let diners know that I do prefer to cook some things differently from what the U.S. Department of Agriculture (USDA) recommends and that anyone with a compromised immune system should take heed. For example, there are few things I enjoy more than a runny egg yolk and few things I like less than tough, overcooked meat and fish. But the USDA suggests you cook yolks through and meats and fish to temperatures I would consider overdone. Along the same lines, many Spanish dishes are served at room temperature. The USDA maintains guidelines on how long different foods should be kept at different temperatures. For detailed information on all of the above, you can read the relevant materials on usda.gov.

# STARTERS

# TOMATO BREAD

In Catalonia, every Spanish meal starts with pan con tomate: toast with olive oil, garlic, and, of course, tomato. It can be eaten alone with a glass of wine or served as part of an appetizer board that includes charcuterie, anchovies, and cheese.

**T**HE TRADITIONAL WAY TO MAKE IT IS SIMPLE. All you have to do is set out toasted split ciabattas or baguettes, halved ripe tomatoes, halved peeled garlic cloves, good extra-virgin olive oil, and salt (a nice, flaky one such as Maldon or fleur de sel, if you have it). Instruct your guests to lightly rub the cut sides of the garlic on the bread (be careful, you can overdo it), then rub and squeeze the cut sides of the tomatoes on the toasted bread hard enough to get a coating of the seeds, juice, and pulp. Drizzle with the oil, sprinkle with salt, and eat! A few people can make it for the whole table or each person can put together her own. The key is to eat it as soon as it's done so the bread stays crisp and the tomatoes juicy.

If you're cooking for a group of eight or more people, this technique can be kind of a pain. A good dinner party trick is the one we use in the restaurant. Make a batch of the Grated Fresh Tomatoes (page 86) the night before. When you're ready to serve, preheat the broiler to high. Slice a large ciabatta loaf in half, splitting it as you would if you were turning it into a sandwich. Place it cut sides up on a half-sheet pan and broil until well-toasted. Flip over and toast the crust sides as well. Flip again and transfer to a cutting board. Immediately spoon the tomato mixture on top, spreading to the very edges of the loaf. Drizzle with olive oil and sprinkle with salt. Cut into pieces and serve.

If you happen to be grilling, you definitely should grill the bread instead of broiling. Pan con tomate goes great with grilled foods or as the accompaniment to any dish. You can even use it as the base for sandwiches (page 223–224). You can't mess up this recipe. The only thing you can do to make it even better is to use the best ingredients you can find.

*El Matrimonio*

## TOMATO BREAD
### WITH ANCHOVIES

DRAPE HIGH-QUALITY ANCHOVIES PACKED IN OLIVE oil and boquerónes (white anchovies marinated in vinegar) over the pan con tomate.

*Tortilla Española*

# SPANISH POTATO, ONION, AND EGG TORTILLA

MAKES ONE 10-INCH TORTILLA; SERVES 4 AS A
MAIN DISH OR 6 TO 8 AS A SMALL PLATE

Tortilla may be Spain's most iconic dish and it's found all over the country. It looks like a frittata, but develops a unique richness with oil-cooked potatoes and onion. The potatoes become tender through a process that hovers somewhere between frying and poaching. Some will turn color, some not, but that's fine as long as they become tender. The onions cook in the same oil and then both go piping hot into the eggs before cooking all together like a giant, thick pancake.

The amount of oil may seem excessive, but it's crucial. The reality is that most of it doesn't get absorbed, but the quantity below is needed to keep the potatoes submerged. You can strain any oil that's left over—it's delicious—and use it to cook anything else. I pour mine into a glass jar with a lid and keep using it until it's gone.

All this may sound intimidating, but tortilla is really forgiving. As long as it browns well on the first side that hits the pan, it's okay if it goes back in ugly after flipping. You can shove it into place and shape it by tucking in the edges with a spatula. As for the flipping itself, choose a board or plate that's a little bigger than the skillet and easy for you to handle. Plates with a lip or rim are even better because they'll keep the egg juices and oil from running out.

Tortilla tastes best at room temperature, making it the ideal do-ahead appetizer. It looks impressive plated whole then sliced to serve and playful when cut in squares and speared with cocktail picks. That's how you'll find it in tapas bars in Spain. Enjoy bites with sips of Oloroso sherry for a magical flavor pairing.

| | |
|---|---|
| **10 large eggs** | **Kosher salt** |
| **1 cup blended oil** | **1 large yellow onion, cut into ¹⁄₁₆-inch slices** |
| **1½ pounds medium Yukon gold potatoes (about 4), peeled and cut into ¹⁄₁₆-inch slices, divided** | |

WHISK THE EGGS IN A LARGE BOWL UNTIL THE yolks and whites are incorporated. Heat the oil in a 10-inch-round, 2-inch-deep well-seasoned cast-iron or nonstick skillet over high heat. When the oil is hot, add half of the potatoes. Flip the potatoes on the bottom to prevent them from browning. Reduce the heat to medium and cover with a lid. Cook until a thin-bladed knife slides through the potatoes easily, 5 to 6 minutes. Use a slotted spoon to transfer the potatoes to the eggs, and stir in 1½ teaspoons salt. Repeat with the remaining potatoes, adding another 1½ teaspoons salt to the eggs when you add the second potato batch.

Pour off all but 2 tablespoons of the oil and reserve. While the oil remaining in the skillet is still hot, add the onion and 1 teaspoon salt. Cook, uncovered and stirring frequently, until the onion is extremely soft, 10 to 15 minutes. If it seems like it may burn, lower the heat. Transfer to the bowl with the eggs and potatoes. Stir until everything is well combined.

Return 2 tablespoons reserved oil to the skillet and reduce the heat to medium-low. Add the egg mixture and spread in an even layer. Cook until the underside is nice and golden, about 10 minutes. If the bottom starts to brown too much before the center starts to set, lower the heat. If the bottom isn't turning golden even as the egg sets, raise the heat for a minute or two to get some color. Remove from the heat.

Loosen the sides of the egg mixture from the skillet by sliding a silicone spatula between the set egg and edge of the pan. You're going to flip the tortilla now. Put on oven mitts and center

*(Continued)*

a large cutting board or flat plate over the pan. Grab the sides of the pan and the cutting board together and flip them, then set them down on the counter. Lift off the pan and put it back on the burner. Carefully slide the tortilla back into the skillet with the pretty golden brown side facing up. Turn the heat to medium.

Run a silicone spatula around the edge of the tortilla, tucking in the edge and rounding it, so it looks pretty again. Cook until the underside is golden, 5 to 6 minutes, adjusting the heat as needed. The timing is going to vary. You can press it with your finger to test for doneness; it should have some give on top and not be super squishy. I never get the same tortillas at home every time. Sometimes I'll hit that perfect runny moment, when the outside is set, but the very center stays wet. Other times, it will be set all the way though. It's delicious either way.

Carefully slide the tortilla out of the pan onto a serving dish. Cool for 1 hour at room temperature. Tortilla Española is best served at room temperature.

Spanish BLT (page 223)

# COCKTAIL SKEWERS

⚓

The term banderillas refers to the sticks used in bull fights, but also translates to "little flags" in Spanish and, more importantly, skewers served with drinks. They're basically the little snacks you'd serve at a cocktail party for a group of friends. The idea is that you're pairing different ingredients into an interesting one-bite combination.

When spearing the ingredients, start with items that might slide off, such as boquerónes, then end with something that will hold at the bottom of the skewer, such as an olive, cornichon, or chunk of Manchego. I don't often put more than three items and usually use only two or even just do a stuffed olive. Think about what people can fit in their mouths.

Though the basis of banderillas is high-quality canned and jarred ingredients, I like to throw in homemade okra pickles. They're so easy and can be done far in advance, and take the tastes to another level. Even if you skip the okra, you can get wonderful results if you follow my formula below, which also works well with green beans and any other vegetables.

You can also make it fun for guests by setting up a DIY banderilla station: Throw a bunch of skewers down with a bunch of ingredients and let your guests try to create the best combo. They get to discover flavors and compare their creations with others (and make it so there's less work for you to do).

What ties these bites together is something bright and refreshing to sip. The Jerez Sour (page 269) would be really good, as would any Fino or Manzanilla sherry.

## PICKLED OKRA

MAKES 2 PINT JARS

| | |
|---|---|
| 9 ounces okra (about 15 small pods) | ¼ teaspoon kosher salt |
| ⅓ cup thinly sliced sweet onion | 2 teaspoons coriander seeds |
| 4 dill sprigs | 1 teaspoon yellow mustard seeds |
| 2 small garlic cloves, peeled | 1 teaspoon dill seeds |
| ½ cup apple cider vinegar | 1 teaspoon black peppercorns |
| ⅓ cup sugar | ½ teaspoon crushed red chile |

**D**IVIDE THE OKRA, ONION, DILL, AND GARLIC among 2 pint jars or containers, packing them in tightly. Heat the vinegar, sugar, salt, and ½ cup water in a small saucepan over medium heat, stirring to dissolve the sugar and salt. Add the coriander seeds, mustard seeds, dill seeds, peppercorns, and chile. Bring to a boil, then divide among the jars.

Cover the jars tightly and cool to room temperature. Refrigerate for at least 1 day or up to 1 week.

### STORE-BOUGHT BANDERILLA ESSENTIALS:

| | |
|---|---|
| anchovies | blue cheese |
| boquerónes | hard Spanish cheeses, such as Manchego, Mahón, Cordobés, Idiazábal |
| olives | |
| piquillos or roasted peppers | |
| | cornichon |
| pickled guindilla peppers | cocktail onions |

*(Continued)*

There isn't a bad combo of stuff. I wouldn't necessarily do blue cheese and Manchego, but I'd put either of those cheeses with anything else. Fatty cheese calms the acidity of olives and pickles. There's no wrong way to go with the ingredients above. Even a boquerón and anchovy, two preparations of the same ingredient, can be paired. In fact, it's called el matrimonio, which means "marriage." That's how well they work together.

olives stuffed with blue cheese (even better wrapped with an anchovy)

olives stuffed with piquillo (even better wrapped with a boqueróne)

anchovies and piquillos

pickled okra and Manchego

guindilla peppers with olives (even better stuffed with blue cheese)

*Croquetas*

# CROQUETTES

MAKES ABOUT 4 DOZEN

Croquetas, a common dish all over Spain, are served hot or room temperature for lunch and dinner or as an appetizer or tapa. Everyone makes them at home and keeps a stash in the cooler. The fillings often come from leftovers ranging from chicken to salt cod. There are a few steps to croquetas, but they can be prepared in stages. And once they're rolled and coated, they can be frozen then fried any time for a 10-minute meal or appetizer. They're best eaten with cold beer; a lager or pilsner would be great.

## HAM CROQUETTES

| | |
|---|---|
| 4 tablespoons unsalted butter | 1½ cups whole milk |
| ½ cup very finely chopped onion | ¼ cup heavy cream |
| ⅓ cup all-purpose flour | 8 ounces very thinly sliced Serrano ham, torn into small shreds |

**M**AKE THE BÉCHAMEL: Melt the butter in a large saucepan over low heat. Add the onion and cook, stirring occasionally, until translucent and soft but not at all browned, about 15 minutes. Add the flour and cook, whisking continuously, just until the raw flour smell dissipates, about 1 minute. Continue whisking while adding the milk a little at a time to prevent the mixture from clumping. Whisk in the cream. Bring to a boil over medium heat, then boil for 2 to 3 minutes, whisking the whole time.

Add the ham and stir for 2 minutes to draw out some of the moisture. Spread the mixture on a half-sheet pan and refrigerate, uncovered, until cold. Shape and fry the croquettes according to the instructions on page 33.

## CHICKEN CROQUETTES

| | |
|---|---|
| 4 tablespoons unsalted butter | 2½ cups finely shredded skinless, boneless Roasted Chicken (page 140) or store-bought rotisserie chicken |
| ½ cup very finely chopped onion | |
| ⅓ cup all-purpose flour | 2 teaspoons kosher salt |
| 1½ cups whole milk | ½ teaspoon freshly grated nutmeg |
| ¼ cup heavy cream | ⅛ teaspoon freshly ground white or black pepper |

**M**AKE THE BÉCHAMEL: Melt the butter in a large saucepan over low heat. Add the onion and cook, stirring occasionally, until translucent and soft but not at all browned, about 15 minutes. Add the flour and cook, whisking continuously, just until the raw flour smell dissipates, about 1 minute. Continue whisking while adding the milk a little at a time to prevent the mixture from clumping. Whisk in the cream. Bring to a boil over medium heat, then boil for 2 to 3 minutes, whisking the whole time.

Add the chicken, salt, nutmeg, and pepper and stir for 2 minutes to draw out some of the moisture. Spread the mixture on a half-sheet pan and refrigerate, uncovered, until cold. Shape and fry the croquettes according to the instructions on page 33.

## MUSHROOM CROQUETTES

| | |
|---|---|
| 2 pounds cremini mushrooms | ½ cup very finely chopped onion |
| ¼ cup extra-virgin olive oil | ⅓ cup all-purpose flour |
| ¼ ounce dried porcinis (⅓ cup) | 1 teaspoon fresh thyme leaves |
| ¾ cup whole milk | ¼ cup heavy cream |
| 4 tablespoons unsalted butter | ½ teaspoon kosher salt |

*(Continued)*

R OAST MUSHROOMS AND MAKE MUSHROOM
stock: Preheat the oven to 350°F. Pulse
the cremini mushrooms in a food processor,
working with 1 pound at a time, until very finely
chopped. Toss with the oil on a half-sheet pan
and spread in an even layer. Roast until browned
and dry, stirring once halfway through, about 45
minutes. Cool completely.

Meanwhile, bring the dried porcinis and 1
cup water to a boil in a small saucepan. Remove
from the heat, cover, and let stand for 15 minutes. Drain through a fine-mesh sieve, pressing
on the solids to extract as much liquid as possible; discard the solids. You should have ¾ cup
stock. Stir the milk into the stock.

To make the béchamel, melt the butter in a
large saucepan over low heat. Add the onion and
cook, stirring occasionally, until translucent and
soft but not at all browned, about 15 minutes.
Add the flour and thyme and cook, whisking
continuously, just until the raw flour smell dissipates, about 1 minute. Continue whisking while
adding the stock-milk mixture a little at a time
to prevent the mixture from clumping. Whisk
in the cream. Bring to a boil over medium heat,
then boil for 2 to 3 minutes, whisking the whole
time.

Add the roasted mushrooms and salt and stir
for 4 minutes to draw out some of the moisture.
Spread the mixture on a half-sheet pan and
refrigerate, uncovered, until cold. Shape and
fry the croquettes according to the instructions
(see sidebar on this page).

## HOW TO SHAPE AND FRY CROQUETTES

| 1 cup panko (Japanese bread crumbs) | ⅓ cup all-purpose flour |
| 1 large egg | Canola oil, for frying |

Roll 1 heaping tablespoon of the cro-
queta mixture into a football shape. It
should be about 2 inches long and 1 inch
in diameter at its thickest point. Repeat
with the remaining mixture. If the mixture
has softened in the process, refrigerate
until firm.

Process the panko in food processor
into fine crumbs, then transfer to a shallow dish. Beat the egg with 1 tablespoon
water in another shallow dish and place
the flour in a third dish.

Working with 4 or 5 pieces at a time,
coat in flour and shake off excess, then
coat with egg and let excess drip off.
Finally, dredge in the panko to completely
cover. Transfer to a wax-paper-lined
half-sheet pan. At this point, you can
cover and refrigerate for up to 3 days
or freeze the coated croquettes. When
frozen rock hard, transfer to airtight containers and freeze for up to 1 month.

When ready to cook, fill a cast-iron skillet
with canola oil to a depth of ½ inch. Heat
over high heat until you see ripples forming on the surface. Drop in one croquette
to test the oil temperature. If it does not
begin to sizzle immediately, then remove
the croquette right away and wait until
the oil gets hot enough. Add just enough
croquette to fit in a single layer without
crowding and reduce the heat to medium.
Fry, using a fork or spoon to carefully turn
the croquettes to brown on all sides, until
golden brown, 3 to 5 minutes. Transfer to
a paper towel-lined plate to drain. Repeat
with the remaining croquettes.

Cool for at least 5 minutes before
serving. You don't want to burn your
tongue, and the croquettes taste great
when completely cooled, too. Serve them
hot, warm, or at room temperature.

*Brandada de Bacalao*

# CREAMY SALT COD AND POTATO SPREAD

MAKES ABOUT 2¾ CUPS;
SERVES 8 TO 10 AS A SMALL PLATE

At Cúrate, we make this traditional Basque Country specialty with a premium desalted bacalao, which is fresh cod that has been salted and dried, then rehydrated and desalinated. It's not available for retail, so making your own salt cod is really important for this dish. While it takes a few days and advanced planning, the steps are simple and the payoff is huge. The salt cod sold in boxes or as stiff planks tends to have a much drier texture, which leads to a grainier brandada. If you make your own bacalao, you end up with a delicious, silky smooth spread that doesn't have an overwhelming fishy flavor. Brandada comes from Basque Country, so bright, crisp Txakoli wine is the ideal pairing. It's bone-dry and lightly carbonated, perfect for cutting through brandada's richness.

1 pound skinless cod fillet

1 cup kosher salt, plus more if needed

1 large Idaho potato, peeled and cut into ½-inch chunks (1½ cups)

7 tablespoons blended oil

12 large garlic cloves, peeled and thinly sliced

1 baguette, cut into ¼-inch slices

Extra-virgin olive oil, for drizzling

CUT THE COD INTO 4 EVEN PIECES AND PLACE IN a container or dish that fits them snugly. Cover with the salt, then cover tightly with plastic wrap. Refrigerate for 48 hours. Rinse the salt off the cod with cold water, rinse the container, and return the cod to the container. Cover the cod with cold water, then cover tightly with plastic wrap. Refrigerate for at least 36 hours and up to 48 hours, changing the water at least 3 times during this process.

Drain the cod well and cut into thin slices. Using your fingertips, shred the slices into small bits and reserve in a bowl.

Place the cut potato in a medium saucepan and cover with cold water by 1 inch. Bring to a boil and cook until fork-tender, about 15 minutes. Drain well and reserve.

Preheat the broiler.

Meanwhile, heat the blended oil in a large saucepan over medium heat. Add the garlic and cook, stirring, just until light golden brown, about 1 minute. Add the reserved salt cod, reduce the heat to low, and cook, stirring often, until the flavors have melded, 15 to 20 minutes.

Transfer to a food processor and add the drained potatoes. Pulse until well-blended, scraping the bowl occasionally. The brandada mixture should be the consistency of soft mashed potatoes. If it's too thick, add a tablespoon or two of water and pulse again. Taste and add salt if needed. It shouldn't need any more salt, but it may, depending on how much salt remains in the cod after it has been cured and soaked. Transfer to a heatproof shallow dish and spread evenly.

Place the baguette slices on a half-sheet pan in a single layer. Drizzle with olive oil. Broil until golden brown, 30 seconds to 1 minute, then flip the slices and broil again, about 30 seconds. The bread goes from golden to burnt in seconds, so check on it often. Cool on the pan.

While the bread cools, broil the brandada in the dish until browned on top, 2 to 3 minutes. Serve hot with the baguette toasts.

# SOUPS AND SALADS

*Gazpacho*

# CHILLED TOMATO, CUCUMBER, AND PEPPER SOUP

MAKES ABOUT 8 CUPS; SERVES 6 TO 8

1 large red bell pepper, seeds and ribs removed, diced, divided

1 large cucumber, peeled and diced, divided

2 pounds super-ripe tomatoes, cored and diced, divided

1 medium garlic clove, chopped, divided

1 cup 1-inch cubes crustless baguette, divided

1 tablespoon sherry vinegar, divided

2 tablespoons dry sherry wine, divided

Kosher salt

½ cup Arbequina extra-virgin olive oil, divided

Gazpacho comes from Andalucía and my version replicates the region's traditional smooth and silky soup. In America, gazpacho has come to mean any type of cold summer soup and is often chunky, laden with all types of summer produce. I prefer the classic trio of tomato, cucumber, and pepper, and my seasonings strike just the right balance between sweet and tart, rounded out by a generous dose of olive oil.

I always make a big, full batch. If it's just for Félix and me, I keep a pitcher of it in the fridge. When we're looking for a refreshing snack on a hot summer afternoon that also provides an energy boost, we drink a cup, sometimes still standing in the kitchen. By the end of the week, the pitcher's empty. If it's for a dinner party, I make it a day or two ahead of time and give it a quick stir before serving. And if it's for the beach or a picnic, I get it super cold, then keep it in a cooler with a spout. That way, anyone can get a cold cup any time while under the sun. The soup is light enough to be a first course before any meal, but also substantial enough for a light lunch with the addition of a salad or bread or both.

YOU NEED TO WORK IN BATCHES TO PUREE THIS soup in standard home blenders: Combine about one-third of the pepper, cucumber, tomatoes, garlic, bread cubes, vinegar, wine, and 1 teaspoon salt with ½ cup water in a powerful blender, preferably a Vitamix if you have one. Puree, gradually raising the speed from low to high. With the machine running, add one-third of the oil in a steady stream, then puree until totally smooth. Strain through a fine-mesh sieve into a large pitcher.

Repeat two more times with the remaining ingredients, using 1 teaspoon salt and ½ cup water for each batch. Taste the mixture and add more salt to taste and more water for the right consistency. It should be drinkable. Depending on how much water your tomatoes are holding, you may need to add another ½ cup water to the strained soup.

Cover tightly and refrigerate at least 4 hours or overnight. When it is very cold, it is ready to serve. Stir well and adjust the seasonings again just before serving.

*Ajo Blanco*

# COLD ALMOND AND GARLIC SOUP WITH CRAB AND GREEN GRAPES

MAKES ABOUT 6 CUPS; SERVES 6 TO 8

Almonds are the nut of Spain. In Málaga, almonds are blended into a creamy white soup. To draw out the almonds' flavor even further for this soup, I break them up with water first, then I soak them to get as much juice as possible out of them. The two-step process makes a big difference in the end result. After that, I just make sure the rest of the seasonings are really well-balanced. The crab and grapes on top turn this into a very satisfying sophisticated first course, but the soup can be drunk on its own, too. In fact, even the almond milk alone is very drinkable. It's far better than any store-bought variety. I tried making this soup with the highest-quality supermarket almond milk I could find and it really didn't work.

The soup, whether served as an appetizer or a light lunch, tastes even better with a glass of wine. A dry Muscatel would be nice, but for the more adventurous, an Amontillado would be even nicer.

1¼ pounds raw almonds

1 cup ½-inch cubes crustless baguette, divided

2 garlic cloves, divided

2 tablespoons sherry vinegar, divided, plus more to taste

Kosher salt

¾ cup extra-virgin olive oil, divided

8 ounces fresh lump crabmeat, picked through for shells and flaked

16 seedless green grapes, sliced crosswise

PULSE THE ALMONDS IN A FOOD PROCESSOR UNtil finely chopped, but not finely ground into a powder. Transfer to a large airtight container and stir in 7 cups cold water. Cover and refrigerate overnight.

Use a measuring cup to scoop 4 cups almond mixture from the bottom of the container into a blender. You want to scoop enough water along with the almonds to get the blender going. Puree until very smooth. A vortex will form in the center and then disappear as the almonds are ground and the mixture thickens. At that point, add more of the water and puree again until very, very smooth, about 2 minutes. It needs the time to get smooth. Repeat with the remaining almonds in 2 more batches.

Pour through a fine-mesh sieve in batches. Stir the mixture in the sieve to help it pass through. You don't want to keep pressing the solids through. When most of the liquid has passed through and the mixture in the sieve looks pasty, discard the solids. You should have 6 cups almond milk. If you have extra, save it for another use. If you don't have enough, add water to make 6 cups.

You need to work in batches to puree this soup in standard home blenders: Combine about half of the almond milk, bread, and garlic with 1 tablespoon vinegar and 1 teaspoon salt in a blender. Process until smooth. With the machine running, add half of the oil in a steady stream. Continue blending until smooth. Strain through a fine-mesh sieve the way you did the almond milk into a large bowl, stirring to let the liquids pass through, but not pressing on the solids. You want to discard the solids while they're still quite wet and pasty to get a very smooth soup without any grainy bits. Repeat with the remaining almond milk, bread, garlic, vinegar, salt, and olive oil, straining into the same bowl. Cover tightly and refrigerate until very cold, at least 4 hours and up to 3 days.

Before serving, whisk well and season with ¼ teaspoon salt and ½ teaspoon vinegar. Taste and add more salt and vinegar if you'd like. Divide among serving bowls and top with the crab and grapes.

_Sopa de Calabaza_

# CREAMY BUTTERNUT SQUASH SOUP

⌇

MAKES ABOUT 9 CUPS; SERVES 8 TO 10

Rather than claiming some Spanish source for this soup, I'll just be honest: The real motivation for this soup was 100% American. I cook Spanish, but I can't escape American traditions to a certain extent. In the fall, Asheville's beautiful as the trees on the endless Blue Ridge Mountain range change colors. With the crisp air, I naturally think butternut squash and cinnamon. It turns out smoked paprika works especially well with that combination, so this soup ended up being Spain-meets-fall-in-the-U.S. This would be a great soup to start Thanksgiving dinner or any autumn meal.

1 teaspoon blended oil

1 whole (2¼-pound) butternut squash, stemmed, cut in half lengthwise, with seeds and pulp scooped out

1 tablespoon unsalted butter

2 small yellow onions (7 ounces), coarsely chopped (2 cups)

3 large carrots, trimmed, peeled, and coarsely chopped (2 cups)

1 cinnamon stick

1 cup heavy cream

4 cups half-and-half, divided

Kosher salt

1 teaspoon smoked pimentón (smoked sweet paprika)

Candied Nuts and Seeds (page 44) made with pepitas (raw hulled pumpkin seeds), for serving

**P**REHEAT THE OVEN TO 350°F. LINE A HALF-SHEET pan with parchment paper.

Rub the oil on the cut sides of the squash to lightly coat. Place the squash halves, cut sides down, on the prepared pan. Bake until caramelized on the cut sides and the skin looks bubbled and golden brown in spots, about 1 hour 25 minutes. The squash should be dark around the edges where the juices have bubbled over. This slow caramelization is really important; you're not just cooking the squash, you're caramelizing it. Let the squash stand until cool enough to handle.

Meanwhile, combine the butter, onions, carrots, and cinnamon stick in a 4-quart saucepan. Set over medium-low heat, cover, and cook, stirring occasionally, until very tender, but not browned, 35 to 40 minutes. You want the carrots to fall apart when you just gently press down on them. Lower the heat as needed to prevent the vegetables from browning.

Use a spoon to scoop out the flesh of the squash while it's still warm into the saucepan with the carrots. Be careful not to get any skin in there, but scrape out as much flesh as you can. Stir well, then add the cream and 3 cups half-and-half. Bring to a simmer over medium heat and simmer, stirring frequently to prevent the dairy from burning, until the mixture is a shade darker in color, about 30 minutes.

Pour half of the mixture into a blender along the back of a spoon to prevent spattering. Puree until smooth, scraping down the sides of the blender occasionally. If the texture isn't smooth enough for you, pass the soup through a fine-mesh sieve. Repeat with the remaining mixture.

Return the soup to the saucepan and whisk in the remaining 1 cup half-and-half. Season with 1½ teaspoons salt, then taste and add more if you'd like. Stir in the smoked pimentón. Serve immediately topped with the Candied Pepitas or refrigerate in airtight containers for up to 1 week. Reheat gently before serving. The soup can't be frozen because pureed soups don't freeze well; they tend to break.

# CANDIED NUTS AND SEEDS

**MAKES 1 CUP**

I sprinkle these on everything, even hot vegetable dishes. Of course, I snack on them alone, too. Rather than coating the nuts or seeds with oil or egg white to get the sugar and salt to stick, I use vinegar. It caramelizes enough to glue on the seasonings, but retains a hint of tartness that makes these taste especially complex.

**1 cup shelled nuts or seeds, such as pepitas (pumpkin seeds) or pine nuts**

**2½ teaspoons white wine, apple cider, or sherry vinegar**

**1 tablespoon granulated sugar**

**½ teaspoon kosher salt**

PREHEAT THE OVEN TO 300°F. LINE A HALF-SHEET pan with parchment paper.

Toss the nuts or seeds with the vinegar in a medium bowl until coated, then toss with the sugar. Spread in a single even layer on the prepared pan. Bake until golden brown and caramelized, about 20 minutes.

Sprinkle with the salt and stir well. Spread in an even layer again and cool completely on the pan on a wire rack. Toss to break into individual pieces. The nuts or seeds can be stored in an airtight container in a cool, dry place for up to 1 week. In heat and humidity, they won't keep for even a day.

_Crema de Setas con Idiazábal_

# CREAMY MUSHROOM SOUP WITH IDIAZÁBAL CHEESE

🌲

**MAKES ABOUT 6 CUPS; SERVES 4 TO 6**

José Andrés, a preeminent Spanish chef with restaurants in America, remains an inspiration years after I started my career in his restaurants. He used to do a cold mushroom soup with Manchego, which I loved so much that I created a hot mushroom soup with Idiazábal cheese for our winter menu at Cúrate. Idiazábal comes from the Basque region, where it's made from the raw milk of Laxta and Carranza sheep. Lightly pressed and aged for under a year, it's supple and creamy with a mild sharpness. To complement that complex cheese, I work the flavor out of the mushrooms by sautéing them for the stock and the base of the soup. But I streamline the rest of the prep. Since the mushrooms are going to be pureed anyway, I don't bother with trimming or finely chopping them. Instead of washing them, I wipe off any dirt with a dry paper towel. The process goes quickly and saves a lot of time later. Mushrooms soak up water like sponges, so if you wash them, they have to release the water first before browning and then take three times as long to sear as dry mushrooms. That little trick yields an intensely flavorful soup that's perfect for chilly days.

## MUSHROOM STOCK

1½ small yellow onions, coarsely chopped (1½ cups)

1 large carrot, scrubbed and coarsely chopped (1 cup)

1 large celery stalk, coarsely chopped (½ cup)

1 large garlic clove, peeled and smashed

2 tablespoons blended oil, divided

1 pound cremini mushrooms, cut in halves (about 6 cups)

1 dried bay leaf

1 (½-ounce) package dried mushroom mix

## MUSHROOM SOUP

2 tablespoons blended oil, divided, plus more as needed

1 pound cremini mushrooms, cut in halves (6 cups), divided

1 small yellow onion, coarsely chopped (1 cup)

2 fresh thyme sprigs, plus leaves for serving

¼ cup dry sherry wine

Kosher salt

Idiazábal cheese, shaved, for serving

Extra-virgin olive oil, for serving

**T**O MAKE THE MUSHROOM STOCK, COMBINE THE onions, carrot, celery, garlic, and 1 tablespoon oil in a 6-quart saucepan. Set over medium-low heat and cook, stirring occasionally, until translucent and soft, about 20 minutes. They should just start to lightly brown in spots and stick to the bottom of the pan.

Add the remaining tablespoon oil, then the cremini mushrooms. Stir well, and cook, stirring occasionally, until tender, about 10 minutes. Add the bay leaf, dried mushrooms, and 8 cups water. Bring to a boil over high heat. Reduce the heat to low and simmer for 1 hour.

Strain through a colander set over another large pot, pressing on the solids to extract as much liquid as possible. You should have 6 cups stock. Bring to a boil over high heat. Reduce the heat to medium and boil until reduced to 4 cups, about 25 minutes.

To make the mushroom soup, heat 1 tablespoon oil in a very large, high-sided cast-iron pan or large skillet over high heat, swirling to coat the bottom of the pan, until just smoking. Add half of the crimini mushrooms in a single, even layer, spacing 1 inch apart, and turn cut sides down.

_(Continued)_

You want the mushrooms to sizzle pretty hard when they hit the pan. Reduce the heat to medium-high and sear until the bottoms are dark golden brown, 3 to 5 minutes. Transfer to a plate. Repeat with the remaining oil and mushrooms. If the pan gets too dry, add just enough oil to cover the bottom of the pan. You want to get the color on there for more flavor. If you add all the mushrooms at once, they'll steam and not brown.

Remove the pan from the heat, then return all the mushrooms to the pan, along with the onion and thyme. Stir well and cook over medium-low heat, stirring occasionally, until the onion is supersoft, about 12 minutes. Reduce the heat if the vegetables start to brown too much.

Add ½ cup mushroom stock, raise the heat to medium-high, and simmer, stirring and scraping the bottom of the pan, until the pan is almost dry, about 7 minutes. Add the sherry and cook, stirring and scraping the bottom of the pan, until almost all the liquid has evaporated, about 2 minutes. Remove from the heat and discard the thyme sprigs.

Transfer to a blender, being sure to scrape all the onions, mushrooms, and juice from the bottom of the pan. Add the remaining mushroom stock. If the blender seems too full, don't add all the stock. Puree until smooth. Pour through a fine-mesh sieve set over another saucepan. If you have any remaining stock, pour through the sieve.

Set over medium-high heat and whisk in 1 teaspoon salt. Reheat until hot. Taste and add more salt if you'd like. I like to season something at the temperature at which I want to eat it. Divide among serving bowls. Scatter the cheese on top, drizzle with olive oil, and sprinkle with the thyme leaves.

*Ensaladilla Rusa*

# RUSSIAN POTATO SALAD

**SERVES 8 TO 10 AS A SMALL PLATE**

Yes, it's called Russian potato salad, but it's distinctly Spanish. Some say it was invented by the Russians in the late nineteenth century, but you can find it in every tapas bar throughout Spain now. In fact, this salad is often used as a measure of how good a place is. If you go into a bar and try it and like it, you should order more food. If not, finish your drink, pay, and move on to the next spot. This version is one that will definitely have everyone at the table staying on for more. It's great on its own as an appetizer or a side dish, but also delicious on toasts.

**ARBEQUINA OLIVE OIL MAYONNAISE**

1 large egg

1½ teaspoons fresh lemon juice

½ teaspoon kosher salt

½ cup blended oil

½ cup Arbequina extra-virgin olive oil

**SALAD**

4 large eggs, shell-on

2 large Idaho potatoes (about 1½ pounds), peeled and cut into ½-inch chunks

Kosher salt

3 medium carrots (about 10 ounces), peeled and cut into ¼-inch dice

½ cup frozen peas

5 canned piquillo peppers, drained, seeded, and cut into ⅛-inch slivers

1 (6½- to 7-ounce) jar tuna packed in olive oil, drained and flaked into ½-inch chunks

TO MAKE THE MAYONNAISE, PROCESS THE EGG, lemon juice, and salt in a food processor until smooth. With the machine running, slowly pour in the oils in a steady stream until emulsified and creamy. Refrigerate in an airtight container while you prepare the salad. The mayonnaise can be refrigerated for up to 1 week.

To make the salad, bring a small saucepan of water to a boil. Add the shell-on eggs, cook for 12 minutes, and then drain immediately. Rinse the eggs under cold water until completely chilled. Peel and cut into ½-inch chunks.

Put the potatoes, 3 cups water, and 1 tablespoon salt in a large saucepan. There should be enough cold water to cover the potatoes. If not, add more. Bring to a boil and simmer for 5 minutes. Add the carrots, return to a boil, then lower the heat to simmer until the potato chunks are soft and the carrots are crisp-tender, 5 to 7 minutes more. Drain very well, then spread out on a half-sheet pan to cool quickly.

Meanwhile, place the frozen peas in a small bowl and cover with hot water. (You can use a ladle of water from the saucepan.) Let stand for 5 minutes, then drain well and add to the pan with the potatoes and carrots.

When the vegetables have cooled, transfer to a large bowl, along with the piquillos, tuna, eggs, and mayonnaise. Using a silicone spatula, carefully fold until everything is well combined. Taste and add more salt if you'd like. Cover tightly with plastic wrap and refrigerate for at least 4 hours or up to 3 days. When ready to serve, let stand at room temperature for half an hour before serving to take the chill off, then fold gently again and season to taste with salt again.

*Ensalada de Endivias
con Queso Azul y Nueces*

# ENDIVE SALAD WITH WALNUTS, POMEGRANATE, AND BLUE CHEESE

**SERVES 8 AS A SMALL PLATE**

When coming up with a winter salad for Cúrate's menu, I turned to a Spanish classic that combines endive with blue cheese and walnuts. To accentuate the nuts, I candy them and make a vinaigrette using roasted walnut oil. (If you can't find roasted walnut oil, you can substitute roasted almond oil. Just be sure the oil is labeled as roasted; otherwise, the flavor doesn't come through.) I had to toss in some pomegranate seeds because they're among my favorite winter fruits; they offer a bright, sweet pop when few other fresh fruits are in season. Also, each of my salads needs something fruity, juicy, and tart to go with my other must-haves: a little crispness and some bitterness, sweetness, and nuttiness.

### CANDIED WALNUTS

1 cup walnut halves

¼ cup sugar

1 tablespoon unsalted butter

¼ teaspoon kosher salt

### WALNUT VINAIGRETTE

2 teaspoons minced shallot

2 tablespoons champagne vinegar

½ cup roasted walnut oil

½ teaspoon kosher salt

⅛ teaspoon freshly ground black pepper

### ENDIVE SALAD

4 heads Belgian endive, trimmed, leaves separated

1 (5-ounce) package mixed greens

1 cup crumbled blue cheese, preferably Spanish, such as Valdeón

Seeds of 1 small pomegranate

TO MAKE THE CANDIED WALNUTS, LINE A HALF-sheet pan with parchment paper. Heat the walnuts, sugar, butter, and salt in a small nonstick skillet or saucepan over medium heat. Cook, stirring constantly, with a silicone spatula. The sugar will melt and begin to caramelize. Once it is a deep amber and just barely beginning to smoke, about 5 minutes, remove the skillet from the heat and immediately scrape the walnut mixture onto the prepared pan. Carefully spread the nuts in a single layer on the pan and cool completely. When cool, coarsely chop into ¼-inch pieces.

Meanwhile, make the vinaigrette. Whisk the shallot and vinegar in a large bowl. Slowly pour in the oil in a steady stream while whisking constantly. Whisk in the salt and pepper.

To assemble the salad, add the endive, greens, blue cheese, pomegranate seeds, and candied walnuts to the bowl with the dressing. Gently toss until everything is evenly coated. Serve immediately.

**TIP:** The best way to get pomegranate seeds out of the fruit is to score a line all the way around its equator, cutting through the skin but not beyond. Use your fingers to pry the halves apart to ensure all the seeds remain intact. Hold a half cut side down in your palm over a bowl and whack the back of the half with a wooden spoon. This act of violence will send the seeds into the bowl below with very little membrane. If any membrane bits fall in, simply pick them out. Repeat with the other half.

*Ensalada de Alcachofas*

# ARTICHOKE SALAD WITH **RADISHES** AND **SALTED YOGURT**

SERVES 4 AS A LIGHT ENTRÉE
OR 8 AS A SMALL PLATE

For this book, I wanted to come up with ways home cooks could re-create Cúrate recipes without the fuss of, say, deep-frying. In the restaurant, we fry paper-thin slices of sunchokes cut with a mandoline to serve as an earthy, crunchy topping. It turns out storebought salted sweet potato chips deliver a just-as-satisfying crispness. And I actually love their sweetness with the acidity of the lemon vinaigrette and the creaminess of the yogurt in this dish. Another shortcut is the use of jarred artichokes. They work well here and make this a 10-minute dish, start to finish. But if you like prepping fresh artichokes, you can do what we do at the restaurant. Once we clean the hearts, we cook them slowly in the lemon vinaigrette. Home-cooked artichokes are more toothsome, but the version here tastes as much of spring.

You can serve this as an appetizer to any spring meal or as a light lunch, along with crusty bread.

## LEMON VINAIGRETTE

1 lemon

1½ teaspoons honey

½ teaspoon kosher salt

¼ cup extra-virgin olive oil

## ARTICHOKE SALAD

½ cup Greek yogurt

Kosher salt and freshly ground black pepper

2 (12-ounce) jars artichokes in water, drained well, then halved lengthwise

8 radishes, very thinly sliced

¼ cup very thinly sliced sweet onion

1 (5-ounce) package spring mixed greens

1 lemon

1 tarragon sprig

¾ cup salted sweet potato chips

TO MAKE THE VINAIGRETTE, ZEST THE LEMON into the bowl of a food processor. Trim the top and bottom of the lemon, then cut off the peel and pith. Holding the lemon flesh over the food processor bowl, cut out the segments by slicing between the membranes. Squeeze any juice remaining in the membranes, then squeeze in any juice in the peel and pith. Add the honey and salt to the bowl and process. With the machine running, add the oil in a slow, steady stream until emulsified. The vinaigrette can be refrigerated in an airtight container for up to 3 days. Bring to room temperature and shake well before using.

To make the salad, stir the yogurt and ¼ teaspoon salt in a small bowl, then spread on serving plates.

Toss the artichokes, radishes, onion, greens, and the vinaigrette in a large bowl. Season to taste with salt and pepper and toss again. Arrange over the yogurt on the serving plates. Zest the lemon and pluck the tarragon leaves over the salad. Scatter the chips on top, breaking larger pieces. Serve immediately.

*Ensalada de Sandía y Tomate*

# WATERMELON TOMATO SALAD WITH GOAT CHEESE AND CORN NUTS

SERVES 8 AS A SMALL PLATE

My chefs and I like to joke that this salad has one ingredient you could source at the gas station. Corn nuts! Before you balk, consider this: Corn nuts are arguably as whole food as junk food gets—they're just corn, oil, and salt. In Spain, they're an enormously popular snack. (If you can find the Quicos ones from Spain, definitely get them.) Even though this salad is all about summery from-the-farm watermelon and tomatoes, the corn nuts make the dish. Their salt and crunch accentuate the juicy sweetness of the fruit. But don't try putting this together any other season; it won't be the same. It's become something we look forward to every summer in the restaurant. While we wait for those heirloom tomatoes, we snack on Quicos in anticipation.

1 tablespoon honey

1½ tablespoons reserve sherry vinegar

Kosher salt

¼ cup extra-virgin olive oil

¼ cup corn nuts, preferably Quicos

4 medium heirloom tomatoes, cut into wedges

4 cups 1-inch watermelon cubes

¼ cup very thinly sliced sweet onion

3 ounces goat cheese, such as Capricho de Cabra

2 tarragon sprigs

WHISK THE HONEY, VINEGAR, AND ½ TEASPOON salt in a small bowl. While whisking, add the oil in a slow, steady stream until emulsified.

Pulse the corn nuts in a food processor until finely chopped.

Arrange the tomatoes in serving dishes in a single layer and sprinkle with ½ teaspoon salt. Top with the watermelon and onion and drizzle with the dressing. Crumble the goat cheese and pluck the tarragon leaves on top. Sprinkle on the corn nuts and serve immediately.

*Ensalada de Remolacha*

# ROASTED BEET SALAD WITH CANDIED ORANGE, MANCHEGO, AND MARCONA ALMONDS

⌄⋏⌃

**SERVES 8 AS A SMALL PLATE**

This salad may not be traditional, but it celebrates autumnal beets using Spanish ingredients. Manchego cheese and salty roasted Marcona almonds go so well with earthy beets. Oranges start rolling into stores in the fall, but aren't quite at the height of sweetness yet, so I candy them to match the orange vinaigrette. Most people don't think they'll hit a winning combination of red wine with salad, but a Rioja or Mencia tastes wonderful with this dish.

**SALAD**

3 medium beets
(1 pound), preferably
1 each red, gold,
Chioggia

3 teaspoons extra-
virgin olive oil,
divided

Kosher salt and
freshly ground black
pepper

1 orange, peel and
pith removed,
segments cut out

4 segments
Candied Oranges
(page 61) cut into
½-inch pieces

2 ounces aged
Manchego cheese,
shaved with a
vegetable peeler

½ cup coarsely
chopped roasted
and salted Marcona
almonds

1 (5-ounce) package
mixed greens

**ORANGE VINAIGRETTE**

1 orange

1½ teaspoons fresh
lemon juice

½ teaspoon minced
shallot

½ teaspoon honey

¼ teaspoon kosher
salt

2½ tablespoons
extra-virgin olive oil

To make the salad, preheat the oven to 400°F.

Peel and cut the beets into 1-inch chunks, keeping the colors separate on different large sheets of foil. Toss each pile of beets with 1 teaspoon oil and a pinch each of salt and pepper. Wrap each mound of beets in the foil to create packets. Place the packets on a half-sheet pan and roast until the beets are tender, 40 to 50 minutes. Unwrap and cool to room temperature.

While the beets roast, make the vinaigrette: Zest one-quarter of the orange into a large bowl, then squeeze in 1½ tablespoons orange juice. Whisk in the lemon juice, shallot, honey, and salt. Slowly pour in the oil in a steady stream while whisking vigorously.

Add the cooled beets, orange segments, candied orange, cheese, almonds, and greens to the bowl with the vinaigrette. Gently toss with your hands until well-mixed. Season to taste with salt and pepper and serve immediately.

# CANDIED ORANGES

MAKES 1½ CUPS

Sevilla is famous for its oranges, which are tart and ideal for preserves. This recipe is my nod to those oranges but can be used with any variety. These easy candied oranges use the whole fruit, not just the peel. That saves you the hassle of scraping off the pith and gives you the benefit of luscious fruit in each bite with the chewy rind. They keep well in the fridge and are delicious with both savory and sweet dishes. They're good with ice cream and can find a place on a cheese plate, too, along with crackers and nuts.

**3 oranges, preferably unwaxed organic**

**1 cup granulated sugar**

**¼ cup white wine vinegar**

**2 whole cloves**

**1 cinnamon stick**

TRIM OFF JUST ENOUGH OF THE TOPS AND BOTTOMS of the oranges to expose the segments. Following the divisions between the segments, cut the oranges from top to bottom into wedges, leaving the rind attached.

Put the orange wedges in a medium saucepan and add enough cold water to cover by 2 inches; bring to a simmer. Simmer, stirring occasionally, for 1 hour.

Strain the oranges through a sieve, return to the same saucepan, and add the sugar, vinegar, cloves, cinnamon, and 3 tablespoons water. Bring to a simmer and simmer gently, stirring occasionally, until the rinds are translucent, about 1 hour 15 minutes. Remove from the heat and cool to room temperature.

Transfer to an airtight jar or container and refrigerate for up to 2 months.

*Ensalada de Atun*

# TUNA AND TOMATO SALAD

SERVES 2 AS A LIGHT ENTREE
OR 4 AS A SMALL PLATE

This classic is so simple, it depends entirely on the quality of the ingredients—both fresh and preserved. You want to find the ripest, juiciest tomatoes, the highest quality tuna (I like Ortiz Bonito del Norte Gran Reserva), and a great extra-virgin olive oil and reserve sherry vinegar. Use your favorite olives, the ones you like to eat on their own. This easy salad is found all over Spain, where home cooks take advantage of the wide variety of great canned tuna found in every market.

To turn this light entrée into a heartier one, add 2 hard-cooked eggs, too.

1 (5-ounce) jar tuna packed in olive oil

8 ounces ripe small Campari or Kumato tomatoes (4 to 6), each cut in 8 wedges

½ cup pitted Kalamata olives

¼ cup very thinly sliced sweet onion

2½ ounces mixed greens

1 tablespoon extra-virgin olive oil

1 teaspoon reserve sherry vinegar

Kosher salt

EMPTY THE JAR OF TUNA INTO A LARGE BOWL. Reserve 1 tablespoon oil in the bowl with the tuna and drain and discard the remaining oil. Flake the tuna, leaving some nice size chunks. Add the tomatoes, olives, onion, greens, olive oil, vinegar, and ¼ teaspoon salt. Toss gently. Taste and add more salt if you'd like. Serve immediately.

# SEAFOOD

*Salpicón de Mariscos*

# CHILLED SHELLFISH SALAD

SERVES 4 AS A MAIN DISH
OR 8 AS A SMALL PLATE

If you go to a really classic tapas bar, you'll see this dish on display, along with croquetas and tortilla. Waiters grab a spoon and drop small mounds as they're ordered. In traditional tapas service, customers can then order a full portion if they've enjoyed their small taste. Even if you're going to dole this out in smaller portions as an appetizer or as part of a larger meal, you're going to want a glass of Albariño wine with it.

It goes without saying that you should find the freshest seafood possible. If it's stone crab season in Florida, you should track down some of those succulent claws. They're my favorite. Otherwise, king crab is nice because of its mild sweetness, or Dungeness with its sea saltiness. Whichever variety you choose, you can easily remove the meat by cutting through the shell with kitchen shears.

Kosher salt

1 fresh or dried bay leaf

5 black peppercorns

3 garlic cloves, 2 smashed and peeled, 1 minced

8 ounces bay scallops

8 ounces small (41/50-count) shrimp, peeled and deveined

3 tablespoons sherry vinegar

3 tablespoons extra-virgin olive oil

¼ cup finely diced red bell pepper

¼ cup finely diced green bell pepper

¼ cup minced onion

8 ounces cooked fresh shell-on crab, meat removed

FILL A LARGE BOWL WITH 2 CUPS ICE, 1 CUP COLD water, and 2 tablespoons salt. Set a colander in the bowl. Combine the bay leaf, peppercorns, smashed garlic, 2 tablespoons salt, and 8 cups water in a large saucepan. Bring to a boil over high heat, then reduce the heat to maintain a low simmer. Add the scallops and cook for 1 minute, then transfer to the colander in the ice bath. Bring the water back to a simmer, add the shrimp, and cook for 30 seconds. Transfer to the colander in the ice bath. When the scallops and shrimp are cold, lift out the colander and let the seafood drain. Reserve the poaching liquid.

Whisk the vinegar in a medium bowl. While whisking, add the oil in a slow, steady stream, then whisk in ¼ cup of the poaching liquid and ½ teaspoon salt. Stir in the red and green peppers, onion, and minced garlic. Taste and add more salt if you'd like.

Combine the scallops, shrimp, crab, and vinaigrette in a large bowl. Gently toss until well-mixed. Cover with plastic wrap and refrigerate for 1 hour. Gently toss again and serve.

*Gambas al Ajillo*

# SAUTÉED SHRIMP
## WITH **GARLIC**

**SERVES 6 AS A MAIN DISH
OR 10 AS A SMALL PLATE**

Gambas rule as our number one tapa. This garlicky shrimp tapa is found all over Spain and is a must-have on our menu. From the day we opened, we discovered how much our diners adore this steaming dish of shrimp swimming in sherried olive oil. Because it combines so few ingredients, proper technique is key. The flavor develops when the garlic browns. We fear burning garlic—justifiably, since it becomes bitter when charred—but when taken to a very deep golden brown, it infuses the sherry-oil sauce with a nearly smoky complexity.

Splurge on the highest-quality shrimp, preferably a fresh, local catch. If you're landlocked, Gulf shrimp from Florida are readily available in supermarkets. What you shouldn't spend a lot on is sherry. Inexpensive dry cooking sherry, such as Taylor or Gibson, is fine. Save the expensive stuff for sipping.

Serve with crusty toasted bread for soaking up all the delicious juices.

2 pounds (26/30-count) shell-on shrimp (about 55)

½ cup blended oil

24 garlic cloves, peeled and thinly sliced

4 fresh bay leaves

6 dried arbol chiles

Kosher salt

1½ cups dry sherry wine

1 tablespoon minced fresh flat-leaf parsley

PEEL THE SHRIMP, LEAVING THE TAIL SHELL intact. Devein the shrimp, then butterfly.

Heat the oil in a large, deep skillet over medium-high heat. Once the oil is hot, add the garlic and cook, stirring, until golden brown, about 1½ minutes. You will want to take this further than you think. We don't want black bits of garlic, but we want them a deep golden brown. Add the shrimp, bay leaves, chiles, and 2 teaspoons salt. Toss the shrimp in the oil until just starting to color, about 2 minutes.

Add the sherry and flip the shrimp so that they cook on all sides. Once the shrimp have turned opaque, immediately transfer them to a bowl, leaving the sauce behind. I usually use tongs to pull each shrimp as it finishes cooking. This is to prevent overcooking the shrimp; it should take only 2 minutes to cook all of them.

Raise the heat to high and boil the sauce until it is reduced and the raw wine flavor of the sherry has diminished, about 1 minute. Return the shrimp to the skillet, add the parsley, and toss quickly to thoroughly coat the shrimp. Transfer the shrimp with its sauce to a serving bowl and serve immediately with crusty toasted bread.

*Almejas a la Sidra*

# CLAMS AND CHORIZO IN CIDER

SERVES 6 AS A MAIN DISH
OR 10 AS A SMALL PLATE

Sidrerías, cider bars, can be found all over the Asturias region, where dry hard apple cider is produced. I love sitting at the bar and watching the servers lift the cider high to pour, intentionally letting it spill all over the floor. That traditional decanting is as fascinating as the unique fruity, funky taste of the cider. In Asturias, it's cooked into a chorizo dish, which I took a step further with the addition of clams and apples. Clams bring a sea-saltiness to the broth, while apples become infused with the cider and add a crunchy sweetness to each bite.

Be sure to use a dry cider with natural carbonation, not the sparkly sweet stuff we're used to in America. I like the Spanish brands Trabanco and Castañon, but what I really love is the surge in craft hard cider in Asheville and all across the United States. Experiment with local dry ciders and buy an extra bottle or two to sip with this dish.

CLEAN THE CLAMS WELL BY RINSING AND scrubbing them under cold water. Throw out any with open, broken, or cracked shells.

Bring the cider to a simmer in a small saucepan, remove from the heat, and add the apple to the hot cider.

Heat the oil in a large lidded saucepot over medium heat. Add the chorizo and cook, stirring, until it begins to turn golden brown, about 2 minutes. Add the shallot, thyme, cinnamon, and bay leaf. Cook, stirring, for 1 minute more. Add the butter and clams to the pot, then strain the cider into the pot, reserving the apple in the strainer.

Raise the heat to medium-high, cover, and bring to a boil. Stir well and reduce the heat to maintain a strong simmer. After 2 minutes, check for any open clams. Pull any that have opened with tongs and place in serving bowls. Stir, and cover again. Keep checking every minute or so, pulling the clams immediately after they open; this will prevent overcooking them.

Once all the clams are in the serving bowls, raise the heat to high and boil the sauce for 1 minute to allow the flavors to develop. Stir in the parsley. There is no salt in this recipe because the natural saltiness of the clams, chorizo, and cider eliminates the need for it. Taste the sauce and add a little salt if you feel it needs it. Discard the thyme, cinnamon, bay leaf, and any clams that don't open.

Pour the sauce over the clams, evenly scraping the chorizo and parsley over all of them. Top with the reserved apple and serve immediately with crusty toasted bread.

50 littleneck clams
(about 7½ pounds)

1 cup dry Spanish
hard cider

½ cup finely diced
peeled sweet-tart
apple, preferably
Honeycrisp

1 tablespoon
blended oil

2 ounces Spanish
chorizo, finely diced

2 tablespoons
minced shallot

2 thyme sprigs

1 cinnamon stick

1 fresh or dried bay
leaf

3 tablespoons
unsalted butter

1 tablespoon minced
fresh flat-leaf parsley

*Mejillones en Escabeche*

# CHILLED MUSSELS IN ESCABECHE SAUCE

⚶

SERVES 4 AS A MAIN DISH
OR 8 AS A SMALL PLATE

Tins of mejillones en escabeche, essentially pickled mussels, line store shelves all over Spain. When Félix served in Spain's army, his go-to cheap eat to avoid mess hall food was a can of this stuff spooned onto a baguette. After he got out of the army, he still ate that combo on lazy Sunday afternoons while watching soccer. I learned this when we were first dating and living in Roses. Because our relationship was relatively new, I enjoyed both the snack and the soccer. Now that we've been married for a while, I can confess that I'm not that crazy about either.

But I knew there could be a delicious version of mussels with a tangy sauce. I liked the idea of a cooked vinaigrette, browning the garlic, onion, and tomato to get a deep richness that wouldn't diminish when cold. The resulting sauce elevates freshly cooked mussels into a great party-worthy cold appetizer.

| | |
|---|---|
| 1 very small ripe tomato | ¾ teaspoon dried thyme leaves |
| 1 large garlic clove, smashed and peeled | ½ fresh or dried bay leaf |
| 3 tablespoons extra-virgin olive oil, divided | 2½ teaspoons reserve sherry vinegar |
| ¼ cup thinly sliced onion | Kosher salt |
| ¾ teaspoon dried rosemary | 2 pounds mussels |

TO MAKE THE ESCABECHE VINAIGRETTE, CUT THE tomato in half and grate the cut side of one half over a bowl using the large holes of a box grater; discard the tomato skin. You need 2 tablespoons pulp and juice. If you don't have enough, grate the other half. If you have too much, save the remaining for another use.

Combine the garlic and 1½ tablespoons oil in a small skillet. Cook over medium heat, stirring, until the garlic is golden brown, about 2 minutes. Add the onion and cook, stirring, until golden brown, about 5 minutes. Add the grated tomato, rosemary, thyme, and bay leaf. Cook, stirring occasionally, until all the liquid has evaporated, about 3 minutes. Add the remaining 1½ tablespoons oil, then stir in ⅓ cup water. Bring to a boil, then adjust the heat to simmer for 5 minutes. Stir in the vinegar and ¼ teaspoon salt. Transfer to a blender to puree until very smooth. Strain through a fine-mesh sieve into a bowl. Cover with plastic wrap and refrigerate until cold, at least 1 hour and up to 1 day.

To clean the mussels, run them under cold water. If their beards stick out from the shells, pull them off and discard. Throw out any mussels with broken shells or ones that will not close when firmly tapped.

Fill a large bowl with 8 cups ice, 4 cups cold water, and ½ cup salt and stir well. Fill a large saucepot with 12 cups water and ½ cup salt. Bring to a rolling boil over high heat and add the mussels. As each mussel pops opens, wait about thirty seconds before completely submerging it in the ice bath. After all the mussels have cooked and cooled, drain and twist off the top shells and discard them. At this point, the mussels can be refrigerated in an airtight container for up to 1 day.

Arrange the mussels on a platter and spoon enough escabeche vinaigrette over each to coat the meat. You want enough vinaigrette to cover the mussel, but not so much that it flows out of the shell.

*Vieiras con Guisantes y Jamón*

# SEARED SCALLOPS WITH PEAS AND HAM

**SERVES 4**

In Spain, peas and jamón are a classic pairing. My added twist is swapping country ham for jamón. That's from my Southern roots. It delivers a bold flavor and texture and it's perfect with sweet peas. In fact, you could make just the ham and pea part of this recipe for a flavorful side dish. I love the addition of seared scallops, though; they cook quickly into an elegant, easy meal, and their salty sweetness complements the ham and peas.

4 tablespoons blended oil, divided

3 ounces country ham, cut into ¼-inch dice (½ cup)

1 large onion, finely chopped (1 cup)

1 garlic clove, minced

1 cup dry white wine

1 pound frozen peas, thawed

Kosher salt

8 large sea scallops, patted dry, tough muscles removed

2 teaspoons chopped fresh mint leaves, plus tiny sprigs for garnish

1 lemon

HEAT 2 TABLESPOONS OIL IN A LARGE, DEEP SKILlet over medium heat. Add the ham and cook, stirring occasionally, until browned and crisp, 4 to 5 minutes. Transfer to a dish. Add the onion to the pan and cook, stirring and scraping up browned bits, until just tender, about 2 minutes, then add the garlic. Cook, stirring until fragrant, about 15 seconds. Add the wine, bring to a boil, then simmer until reduced by half. Add the peas and browned ham and simmer just until the peas are heated through, 1 to 2 minutes. Stir in ½ teaspoon salt, then keep warm over low heat.

Heat the remaining 2 tablespoons oil in a large skillet until very hot. Season the scallops with salt and add to the hot oil. Cook, turning once, until deeply browned and seared, 1 to 2 minutes per side. Transfer to serving plates.

Fold the mint into the warm peas and divide among the plates. Garnish with the mint sprigs and zest the lemon directly on top. Serve immediately.

*Pulpo a la Gallega*

# OCTOPUS WITH OLIVE OIL AND PIMENTÓN

---

**SERVES 4 AS A MAIN DISH
OR 8 AS A SMALL PLATE**

In Galicia, octopus is served at celebrations and often cooked outdoors in huge metal drums. At home, you can create the same effect with a stockpot. To make it a la gallega, you simply drizzle it with olive oil and sprinkle it with pimentón just before serving. It's important that you buy wild octopus from Spain or Portugal because other varieties may not end up as soft and succulent. The tentacles become super tender after a boil with aromatics. You can find cleaned octopus at well-stocked seafood counters and buy it frozen if that's the only form in which it's sold. Simply thaw overnight in the refrigerator. This octopus dish tastes best when served with the Olive Oil Potato Puree (page 165) but it's delicious on its own, too.

**1 cup kosher salt**

**2 fresh or dried
bay leaves**

**20 black
peppercorns**

**1 whole (3-pound)
fresh wild octopus
from Spain or
Portugal, beak
removed**

**Extra-virgin olive oil,
for drizzling**

**Pimentón (smoked
sweet paprika),
for dusting**

**Maldon sea salt,
for sprinkling**

FILL A VERY LARGE STOCKPOT WITH 8 QUARTS water. Add the salt, bay leaves, and peppercorns and bring to a boil. Once the water is at a rolling boil, hold the octopus by its head and dunk its tentacles into the boiling water. Holding it by its head, keep the tentacles submerged for 10 seconds. Lift out the octopus and hold it above the pot for 10 seconds. Repeat this process a total of six times. The dunking prevents the tentacles from curling up tightly, which makes them difficult to slice after cooking.

After the sixth time, submerge the octopus in the boiling cooking liquid. Reduce the heat to maintain a slow and steady but not rolling boil. Cook until the octopus is very tender, about 1 hour.

Carefully remove the octopus from the cooking liquid and place on a large cutting board; reserve the cooking liquid if you're making this dish ahead of time. When it's cool enough to handle, remove the head by cutting horizontally across the neck and discard it. Carefully cut the tentacles into individual tentacles.

If you're making this ahead of time, transfer the tentacles to a large airtight container. Add enough of the cooking liquid to cover. Cover tightly and refrigerate for up to 2 days. Discard the remaining cooking liquid.

If you're serving immediately, cut the tentacles into ¼-inch slices. Transfer to serving dishes in a single layer. Drizzle with oil to generously coat. Dust with pimentón and season with a bit of salt. Serve immediately.

If you've cooked the octopus ahead of time, preheat the broiler when you're ready to serve.

Remove the tentacles from the cooking liquid and cut into ¼-inch slices. Pat dry, then transfer to a shallow ovenproof baking or casserole dish and arrange in a single layer. Drizzle with oil to generously coat.

Broil until warmed through, about 5 minutes. Very carefully remove from the broiler. Dust with pimentón and season with a bit of salt. Serve immediately.

# PREPARING OCTOPUS

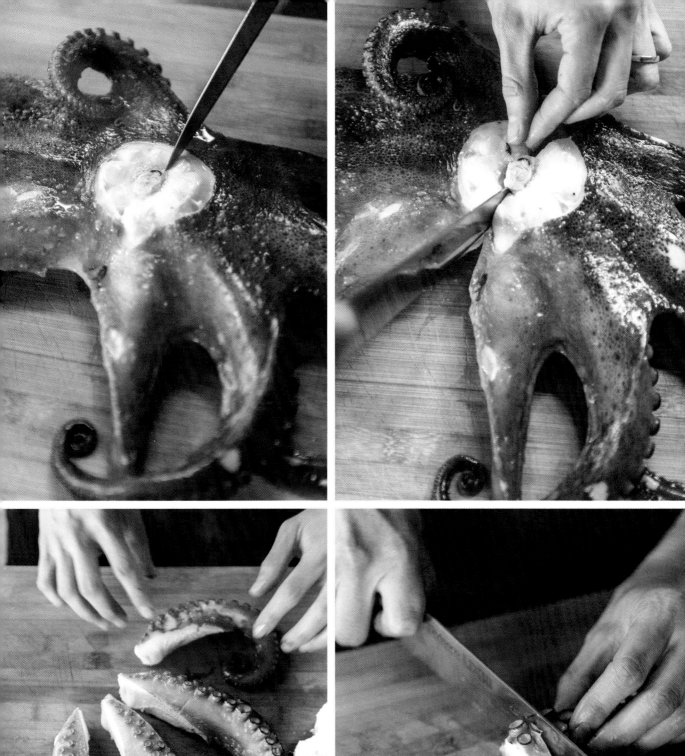

*Calamares Rellenos*

# STUFFED SQUID IN MANZANILLA TOMATO SAUCE

⌁

**SERVES 4 AS A MAIN DISH OR 8 AS A SMALL PLATE**

Mushrooms are a staple of both Catalonia and North Carolina's mountains, so I wanted to showcase them in this classic Spanish tapa, which is normally stuffed with only squid, aromatics, and bread crumbs. Mushrooms bring as much depth to the dish as my technique of caramelizing the vegetables for the sauce. Since the whole process is pretty labor-intensive, I use a food processor to chop the vegetables for the sauce. They need to be cut small to brown well, but they don't have to look pretty. If you want, you can use the machine to cut the squid, onion, garlic, and mushrooms for the filling, too. The mixture will end up smoother and firmer but still taste wonderful.

**MANZANILLA TOMATO SAUCE**

1 pound onions (3 medium), peeled and coarsely chopped

4 small carrots, peeled and cut in chunks

2 tablespoons canola oil

4 garlic cloves, crushed and peeled

1 (14.5-ounce) can crushed San Marzano tomatoes

2 cups Manzanilla sherry wine

**STUFFED SQUID**

1 pound squid bodies and tentacles, cleaned, divided

3 tablespoons plus 2 teaspoons canola oil, divided

1 medium onion, finely chopped (1 cup)

3 large garlic cloves, minced

5 ounces cremini mushrooms, trimmed and finely chopped (1 cup)

(STUFFED SQUID continued)

1 thyme sprig

½ cup Manzanilla sherry wine

¼ cup panko (Japanese bread crumbs)

1 tablespoon minced fresh flat-leaf parsley leaves

Kosher salt

Toothpicks, for skewering

TO MAKE THE MANZANILLA TOMATO SAUCE, pulse the onions and carrots in a food processor until finely minced, scraping the bowl occasionally. It's okay if the pieces aren't perfectly uniform because the vegetables are strained out later. Heat the oil in a large skillet over medium-high heat. Add the garlic and cook, stirring, until golden brown, about 30 seconds. Add the minced carrots and onions and cook, stirring occasionally, until all the liquid has evaporated and the vegetables have begun to caramelize, about 10 minutes.

Add the crushed tomatoes and cook, stirring occasionally, until the liquid has evaporated and the tomatoes begin to caramelize, about 5 minutes. Stir in the sherry, scraping up any browned bits. Simmer for 5 minutes, then strain through a fine-mesh sieve, pushing firmly on the solids to extract as much liquid as possible. Reserve. The sauce can be refrigerated in an airtight container for up to 5 days.

Meanwhile, make the stuffed squid. If the squid bodies are still attached to the tentacles, cut them apart. If the bodies still have the stiff cartilage spine inside, remove and discard. If the bodies still have the outer wings attached, carefully pull them away. Pack the wings and tentacles into a ½ cup measuring cup; if it isn't full, add enough of the smallest bodies to fill it. Transfer to paper towels and squeeze very dry. You should have about 12 bodies remaining; refrigerate them.

Heat 2 tablespoons oil in a large skillet over medium-high heat until hot. Add the squid wings, tentacles, and any bodies with them. Be careful; the squid may pop out of the pan and the oil may splatter if there's any water on the squid. Cook, turning to evenly brown, until well-seared, 2 to 3 minutes. Transfer to a cutting board. Add

*(Continued)*

1 tablespoon oil to the skillet, reduce the heat to medium, and add the onion and garlic. Cook, stirring and scraping up the browned bits, until glassy, about 8 minutes. While the onion mixture cooks, very finely chop the seared squid. Return the squid to the pan and add the mushrooms and thyme. Raise the heat to medium-high and cook, stirring often, until the mixture is very dry and begins to slightly brown and stick to the pan, about 5 minutes. Add the sherry and cook until all the liquid evaporates. Remove from the heat and discard the thyme. Stir in the panko, parsley, and ½ teaspoon salt. Spread out on a plate and refrigerate to quickly cool room temperature.

Transfer the cooled squid mixture to a heavy-duty resealable plastic bag. Snip a ½-inch hole in one corner, essentially making a piping bag. Stick the corner with the hole cut out into the opening of a reserved squid body and squeeze in the squid filling until the body is about two-thirds full. Repeat with the remaining squid bodies and filling. Use a chopstick or the dull end of a skewer to push the filling into the body to remove any air pockets. Seal the open ends of the squid bodies with a toothpick using a sewing motion. The stuffed squid can be covered tightly with plastic wrap and refrigerated for up to 1 day.

Heat the remaining 2 teaspoons oil in a large skillet over high heat until very hot. Lightly season the stuffed squid with salt and add to the hot oil. Cook, turning once, until golden, about 2 minutes per side. Reduce the heat to medium and add the tomato sauce. Simmer until the sauce has thickened enough to coat the squid.

Transfer the squid to a serving platter and carefully remove the toothpicks. Pour the sauce all over and serve hot.

*Sardinas a la Brasa*

# GRILLED SARDINES

Grilled sardines represent the best of coastal Spanish cuisine. All you need for the day's catch are olive oil, salt, and fire. If you're lucky enough to live somewhere with a fish monger who can sell you the day's catch, become friends with her and start cooking. Look for sardines with bright, shiny eyes and skin and ask the fishmonger to gut them for you.

**Olive oil**              **Salt**

**Sardines, fresh**

AS SOON AS YOU GET HOME, RUB YOUR GRILL grate with a paper towel dampened with olive oil. Get your grill really hot with the coals on one side of it. Season the sardines with a little salt inside and out, and rub them with a sheen of olive oil. The key to keeping the fish from sticking to the grate is getting the grate super-hot first; when it's ready, put the fish on it, right next to the coals but not directly above them. If they're right over the coals, their dripping juices will cause flare-ups. Flames hitting the fish can create an acrid taste.

Once the sardines are on, don't touch them. Flip them only when they release from the grate easily; minutes will have gone by. Once turned, they should cook only until their flesh is opaque throughout, which you can see by peeking in the centers. Don't overcook them. The skin on the second side may stick, so you may end up with one presentation side and one stuck side, but that's okay—it's better than ending up with dry fish. Eat them while they're hot and their skin is blistered and crisp.

*Esqueixada de Montaña*

# CURED TROUT WITH TOMATO, BLACK OLIVE, AND ONION

**SERVES 4 AS A MAIN DISH OR 8 AS A SMALL PLATE**

Esqueixar means "to shred" and that's what's done to salt cod in this traditional Catalonian cold dish. I'm using trout instead, which is as prevalent in Asheville as it is in Spain. For the restaurant, we get fresh trout delivered the day it is caught and serve it raw. Since I'm not sure everyone can get trout that fresh, I lightly cure it here to retain its silky tenderness. (Note that the trout is cured, not cooked, if you're concerned about consuming raw fish.) Since the fillets aren't as flaky as cod, they don't get shredded. In thin slices, though, they capture the spirit of esqueixada.

### GRATED FRESH TOMATOES

2 large super-ripe tomatoes (10 ounces)

2 garlic cloves, minced

1 large rosemary sprig

1 teaspoon kosher salt

½ cup extra-virgin olive oil

### CURED TROUT

1 pound trout fillets, pin bones removed

¼ cup gin

8 juniper berries, crushed with the flat side of a knife

1 teaspoon black peppercorns, crushed

½ cup kosher salt

½ cup granulated sugar

### SALAD

3 tablespoons Lemon Vinaigrette (page 53)

¼ cup thinly sliced sweet onion

¼ cup diced pitted Kalamata olives

1 lemon

TO MAKE THE GRATED FRESH TOMATOES, CUT the tomatoes in half through their equators. Set a box grater over a large bowl. Grate the cut sides of the tomatoes on the large holes until only the skin remains; discard the skins. Stir in the garlic. Cut the rosemary sprig in half, then bruise the sprigs by gently pounding with the dull edge of a knife and add to the tomato mixture. Whisk in the salt and oil. Cover tightly with plastic wrap and refrigerate overnight for the flavors to meld.

To make the cured trout, find a container or shallow dish just large enough to hold the fillets snugly in a single layer. Line the container with plastic wrap with overhang on all sides. Place the fillets in the plastic wrap, skin side down. Pour the gin on top. Mix the juniper, peppercorns, salt, and sugar in a small bowl, then spread over the fillets to evenly coat. Cover with the plastic wrap overhang and then cover the whole container with plastic wrap. Refrigerate for 4 hours.

Unwrap the trout, rinse off the cure under cold water, and pat dry. Cut the trout off the skin; discard the skin. Cut the fillets into ⅛-inch-thick slices. Remove the rosemary from the tomatoes and spread the tomatoes on a serving platter. Top with the trout slices. Drizzle the lemon vinaigrette on top, then sprinkle with the onion and olives. Zest the lemon directly on top and serve immediately.

*Trucha con Jamón Ibérico*

# SEARED HERB-STUFFED TROUT WRAPPED IN IBÉRICO HAM

SERVES 2 AS A MAIN DISH
OR 4 AS A SMALL PLATE

Trout are cooked and eaten anywhere they're caught in Spain, in river regions from north to south and east to west. I took one of my favorite Spanish preparations and brought freshness by stuffing the cavity with herbs. They infuse the flesh with their aromas while the ham creates a crunchy porky skin. I originally attempted an American twist by swapping in bacon for the ham, but it doesn't crisp quite as nicely. By the time the strips cook through, the trout tends to be over-cooked. Turns out the original was definitely the way to go.

1 whole (12-ounce) trout, gutted and scaled

Kosher salt

2 lemon wheels

2 rosemary sprigs

6 thyme sprigs

2 to 4 ounces very thinly sliced ham, Ibérico or Serrano

2 tablespoons blended oil

SEASON THE TROUT INSIDE AND OUT WITH 1 teaspoon salt. Lay the lemon wheels inside in the cavity and top with the rosemary and thyme. Wrap the trout with the ham, overlapping the slices slightly and completely covering the fish and enclosing the lemon and herbs. The stuffed and wrapped trout can be cooked immediately or refrigerated for up to 4 hours.

Heat the oil in a large skillet over medium heat. Add the trout and sear until the bottom is nicely browned, 3 to 4 minutes. Carefully flip the fish and sear the other side, 3 to 4 minutes.

Transfer to a serving plate and let rest for a few minutes. Cut the fillets with the ham off the bone, season to taste, and serve.

*Bacalao con Tomate*

# FRESH COD WITH TOMATO SAUCE AND GARBANZOS

SERVES 4 AS A MAIN DISH
OR 8 AS A SMALL PLATE

Seafood stock intensifies this chunky, smoky tomato sauce with a deep savory note ideal for the fresh seared cod. The addition of earthy garbanzo beans turns this into a hearty, warming dish. Even though this whole meal comes together quickly, it tastes like it's developed its deep flavors over many hours. Be sure to serve it with rice or good bread for sopping up the sauce.

3 tablespoons extra-virgin olive oil, divided

8 garlic cloves, peeled and sliced

½ cup finely chopped onion

1 cup canned crushed tomatoes

1 fresh or dried bay leaf

1 small rosemary sprig

1 cup seafood stock, homemade (page 183) or store-bought unsalted stock

1 (14.5-ounce) can garbanzo beans (chickpeas), rinsed and drained

1 teaspoon pimentón (sweet smoked paprika)

1 tablespoon minced fresh flat-leaf parsley

Kosher salt

4 (6-ounce) skinless cod fillets

HEAT 1 TABLESPOON OIL IN A LARGE SAUTÉ PAN over medium-low heat. Add the garlic and cook, stirring, until golden, about 30 seconds. Add the onion and cook, stirring, until almost translucent, about 5 minutes. If the onion begins to brown, add a splash of water. Add the tomatoes, bay leaf, and rosemary. Reduce the heat to low and cook, stirring occasionally, until the liquid has evaporated, about 5 minutes. Add the seafood stock, garbanzo beans, and pimentón. Raise the heat to bring to a boil, then reduce the heat to low and simmer for 5 minutes. Discard the bay leaf and rosemary. Stir in the parsley, season with ¼ teaspoon salt, remove from the heat, and reserve in the pan.

Heat the remaining 2 tablespoons oil in a large nonstick skillet over high heat. Season the fish with 1 teaspoon salt on both sides. Add to the pan, smooth side down. Cook until golden brown and the flesh releases easily from the pan, about 3 minutes. Carefully turn the fillets over. Add the tomato garbanzo mixture to the skillet and cook until the fish is just opaque throughout and the sauce is bubbling, about 4 minutes. Serve the fish with the sauce spooned all around.

*Pescado Frito en Adobo*

# ADOBO FRIED FISH

---

SERVES 4 AS A MAIN DISH
OR 8 AS A SMALL PLATE

I really love the vinegary flavor in the fried fish here. It's a surprising contrast where you're not really expecting it. Traditionally, this dish is made with cazón, known as "dogfish," which has meaty, firm white flesh. I've tried it with grouper and orange roughy, too. Any white fish that can hold its shape in chunks when fried will work here.

4 piquillo peppers

2 teaspoons ground cumin

1 teaspoon pimentón (smoked sweet paprika)

1 teaspoon freshly ground black pepper

Pinch cayenne pepper

¼ cup white wine vinegar

2 tablespoons packed fresh flat-leaf parsley leaves

2 tablespoons packed fresh oregano leaves

3 garlic cloves, peeled

Kosher salt

Arbequina Olive Oil Mayonnaise (page 49)

1½ pounds skinless grouper, orange roughy, or other firm white fish fillets, cut into 1½-inch chunks

⅓ cup all-purpose flour

Canola oil, for frying

IN A FOOD PROCESSOR OR BLENDER, COMBINE THE piquillos, cumin, pimentón, black pepper, cayenne pepper, vinegar, parsley, oregano, garlic, 1 teaspoon salt, and 1 tablespoon water. Puree until smooth, scraping the bowl occasionally. The adobo mixture should be thick enough to stick to the fish but not be stiff and pasty. If needed, blend in another tablespoon water. Transfer half of the adobo mixture to a bowl and stir in the mayonnaise. Cover and refrigerate until ready to serve. Transfer the remaining adobo sauce to another large bowl. The adobo and adobo mayonnaise can be refrigerated in airtight containers for up to 3 days.

When ready to serve the dish, season the fish chunks on all sides with salt, toss in the bowl with the adobo to completely coat. Place the flour in a shallow dish.

Fill a large skillet with oil to a depth of ¼ inch. Heat over medium-high heat until hot but not smoking. While the oil heats, dredge a few fish chunks in the flour and shake to remove excess flour. Add to the hot oil and cook, turning once, until golden brown and cooked through, about 5 minutes. Drain on paper towels. Repeat with the remaining fish. Serve with the adobo mayonnaise for dipping.

# HAKE AND CLAMS WITH PARSLEY SAUCE

SERVES 4 AS A MAIN DISH
OR 8 AS A SMALL PLATE

The classic preparation of this dish uses only fish, but I added clams and clam juice to give the whole thing more body. In the restaurant, we use homemade seafood stock (page 183). If you happen to have some on hand, use it in place of the clam juice. It'll taste even more luxurious.

20 littleneck clams (about 3 pounds)

1 tablespoon extra-virgin olive oil

2 tablespoons minced shallot

1 tablespoon minced garlic

½ cup dry white wine, preferably Albariño

1 cup bottled or canned clam juice, divided

4 tablespoons blended oil, divided

4 (6-ounce) skinless hake or cod fillets

1½ tablespoons all-purpose flour

2 tablespoons minced fresh flat-leaf parsley

CLEAN THE CLAMS WELL BY RINSING AND scrubbing them under cold water. Throw out any with open, broken, or cracked shells.

Heat the olive oil in a large saucepan over medium-high heat. Add the shallot and garlic and cook, stirring until fragrant but not brown, about 1 minute. Add the clams, wine, and ½ cup clam juice. Cover and steam until all the clams open. After 3 minutes, check for any open clams. Pull any that have opened with tongs and place in a bowl. Stir and cover again. Keep checking every minute or so and pulling the clams immediately after they open. This will prevent overcooking the clams. Reserve the steaming liquid.

Heat 2 tablespoons blended oil in a large, deep nonstick skillet over high heat. Add 2 hake fillets and sear, turning once, until golden brown, about 2 minutes per side. Transfer to a plate. Repeat with the remaining blended oil and fish.

Reduce the heat to low and whisk in the flour. Be ready with your remaining ½ cup clam juice because the sauce comes together fast. Keep whisking the flour-oil mixture until it starts to barely turn golden. We aren't looking for any dark color here. Carefully but quickly whisk in the remaining clam juice to stop the mixture from cooking any further. Whisk in the reserved clam cooking liquid. Keep cooking and whisking until the sauce is reduced enough to lightly coat the back of a spoon, about 5 minutes.

Return the fish to the skillet and simmer, turning once, until just opaque throughout, about 2 minutes. Transfer the fish to serving plates. Stir in the parsley, then toss in the clams with their accumulated juices to heat through. Spoon the clams and sauce onto the plates with the fish. Serve immediately.

# MEAT AND POULTRY

*Albóndigas con Jamón y Tomate*

# MEATBALLS WITH SERRANO HAM IN TOMATO SAUCE

SERVES 6 TO 8 AS A MAIN DISH
OR 10 TO 12 AS A SMALL PLATE

One of the first dishes Félix's mom, Pepa, made for me was albóndigas. They were the best meatballs I'd ever had. They were so tender, they fell apart the second I put them in my mouth. One bite and I could see why they were Félix's favorite and why everyone in his family talked about Pepa's albóndigas all the time. Félix grew up helping Pepa roll them, standing on a step stool at the counter. She'd feed them to him, one by one, as soon as they came out of the pan, even before they went into the sauce. From the moment I tasted them, I knew I had to have albóndigas on Cúrate's menu.

I spent over a year experimenting with my albóndigas recipe, and in the process I added my unique twist: ham. It started as a way to avoid wasting food. We had all these scraps of Ibérico ham from assembling our charcuterie plates and wanted to figure out how to use them. The answer was mixing the bits into the pork-and-beef mixture and making a stock with the bone. Assuming you don't have ham bones at home, I've adapted the stock recipe for sliced ham. In fact, you can do this with Southern country ham, too—just season a lot less, because country ham is much saltier. Rosemary is my other addition. It's not used in albóndigas, but it does grow all over Catalonia. Its piney fragrance simultaneously matches and balances all the fatty meat. Good meatballs are as much about texture as they are about taste. To that end, I make sure all

the vegetables are minced and cut the bread in tiny cubes. Finely dicing the bread creates more space between the dense meat mixture, makes the fried balls light and airy inside.

Serve with good, crusty bread or over pasta or rice. The albóndigas are filling enough to be a main dish that needs only a simple green salad on the side. They also work well as a party dish. Simply spear them with cocktail skewers to serve as an appetizer.

1 tablespoon blended oil

1¼ cups minced onions (from about 2 small yellow onions)

1 tablespoon plus 1 teaspoon packed minced garlic (from about 6 cloves)

¼ cup dry white wine

¼ cup Jamón Stock (page 101)

2 cups ⅛-inch cubes crustless stale ciabatta (from about 1½ small rolls)

5 ounces Serrano ham (10 very thin slices), very finely chopped

½ pound ground beef chuck (80/20 fat)

½ pound ground pork (85/15 fat)

1 large egg

2 large egg yolks

¼ cup minced fresh flat-leaf parsley leaves

1½ teaspoons kosher salt

¾ cup all-purpose flour, for dusting

4 cups Tomato Sauce (page 100) warm or room temperature

Canola oil, for frying

HEAT THE OIL IN A LARGE CAST-IRON OR OTHER heavy skillet over medium-high heat. Add the onions and spread in an even layer. Once the onions start to sizzle, reduce the heat to medium-low. Cook, stirring frequently, until just softened and shiny, about 5 minutes. Stir in the garlic. Cook, stirring frequently, until golden and fragrant, 1 to 2 minutes.

Add the wine and ham stock. Raise the heat to medium-high and bring to a simmer. Cook until the liquid is reduced by half. You want to cook out the wine, but keep some liquid in there for the bread to soak and get soft. Remove from the heat, add the bread cubes, and stir well to evenly coat and let it soak up the liquid.

*(Continued)*

Transfer to a large plate and spread in an even layer to cool completely. If you're in a rush, transfer to the freezer to cool to room temperature quickly.

Meanwhile, break up the ham into tiny pieces in a large bowl. The fat tends to stick to itself, so you need to separate the pieces again after cutting to avoid getting any big clumps of salty ham. Add the ground beef and pork and break apart to evenly distribute with your fingers. Beat the egg and egg yolks until blended in a small bowl. Add to the meat, along with the parsley, salt, and onion mixture. Mix with your hands until thoroughly combined.

Roll 1 rounded tablespoon of the mixture into an albóndiga. It should be the size of a Ping-Pong ball. Repeat with the remaining mixture to make 36 albóndigas. If you have time, refrigerate them first and let them get cold. They're easier to fry and hold their shape when cold. The uncooked albóndigas can be refrigerated in an airtight container for up to 3 days.

When ready to cook, preheat the oven to 375°F. Place the flour in a medium bowl. Drop an albóndiga into the flour, turn to coat, then lift out and reroll in your hands, shaking off excess flour while you roll. Transfer to a clean plate or pan. Repeat with the remaining albóndigas.

Put the tomato sauce in a large Dutch oven or other heavy ovenproof saucepot with a lid. If you're starting with cold tomato sauce from the fridge, reheat it to warm first.

Fill a large cast-iron skillet with canola oil to a depth of ½ inch (about ½ cup). Heat over high heat until an instant-read thermometer registers 350°F. When you drop an albóndiga in the oil, it should sizzle immediately and brown.

Add only as many albóndigas as can fit in a single layer with 2 inches between the balls. You don't want to crowd the pan. Cook, turning occasionally with tongs, to evenly brown, 3 to 5 minutes. You're going for a dark golden brown. As the albóndigas finish browning, transfer them to the tomato sauce. Repeat with the remaining albóndigas. The later batches will go faster because the oil gets hotter and they'll also brown faster because the oil is darker. When you're done cooking, you'll have to dump this oil because of all the flour in it.

Make sure all the albóndigas are covered with the sauce, gently spooning the sauce over them and pushing them down if needed. Cover the Dutch oven and bake for 45 minutes. Serve hot.

*Salsa de Tomate*

# TOMATO SAUCE

### MAKES 4 CUPS

This recipe is the reason I own a food mill. It squeezes all the sauce out and leaves the seeds and rosemary leaves behind. You really want the sauce to be smooth so that it can cling to Albóndigas (page 99). It's also a handy all-purpose tomato sauce for pasta.

2 (28-ounce) cans whole peeled San Marzano tomatoes

1 tablespoon plus 1 teaspoon blended oil, divided

1 small yellow onion, very thinly sliced (1 cup)

6 small garlic cloves, peeled and sliced

2 tablespoons tomato paste

¼ cup dry red wine

1 rosemary sprig

¼ cup Jamón Stock (page 101)

Kosher salt

2 tablespoons extra-virgin olive oil

REMOVE THE TOMATOES FROM THEIR LIQUID IN the cans; reserve the liquid. Coarsely chop the tomatoes and transfer to a large bowl. Add the reserved tomato liquid from the cans.

Heat 1 tablespoon blended oil over medium heat in a large stockpot or Dutch oven. Stir in the onion. Once it starts to sizzle, reduce the heat to low. Cook, stirring occasionally, until tender and translucent but without any color, about 10 minutes. If the pan starts to get too dry or if you notice the onions starting to take on any color, stir a little water into the pan.

Push the onions to one side of the pan and add the remaining teaspoon blended oil to the other side. Add the garlic to the oil and cook, stirring, until softened and fragrant, about 2

*(Continued)*

minutes. Push to the side with the onions. Add the tomato paste to the other side and raise the heat to medium-low. Cook, stirring, until the paste starts to stick and caramelize but not burn on the bottom, about 1 minute. Stir into the onion-garlic mixture, then pour in the wine. Cook, stirring and scraping the bottom of the pot, until the liquid has almost all evaporated, about 1 minute. Add the rosemary, tomatoes with their juices, and ham stock. Bring to simmer over medium-high heat. Reduce the heat to maintain a low simmer and simmer, stirring occasionally, until you can no longer taste the acid in the tomatoes and the mixture has thickened, about 3 hours. You have to cook for a really long time for the flavors to intensify and sweeten.

Discard the rosemary, then pass the sauce through a food mill or puree it in a food processor or blender until smooth. Stir in ½ teaspoon salt and the olive oil. Taste and add more salt if you'd like. You should have 4 cups sauce. If you're using it right away, return to a large saucepan or Dutch oven. Otherwise, you can keep the sauce in an airtight container in the fridge for 1 week or in the freezer for months.

# JAMÓN STOCK

MAKES ½ CUP

**3 ounces Serrano ham
(6 very thin slices),
finely chopped**

COMBINE THE HAM AND 1 CUP COLD WATER IN A small saucepan. Stir to break the ham apart and submerge in the water. Bring to a simmer over medium heat. Adjust the heat to maintain a very low simmer for 12 minutes because you don't want to evaporate the water. Strain through a fine-mesh sieve, pressing on the solids to extract as much liquid as possible. You should have ½ cup stock. Reserve half for the Tomato Sauce (page 100), and half for the Albóndigas (page 99). Discard ham.

*Filete de Ternera a la Brasa*

# GRILLED SPICE-RUBBED HANGER STEAK

SERVES 4

I love charred hanger steak. This budget cut of meat has a complex beefiness that needs little more than salt and pepper, but my instant spice rub adds a welcome complexity. The rub isn't traditional in Spain, but it's my way of combining Spanish and Moorish seasonings in the distinctly American main dish of grilled steak. The combination of pimentón and cayenne pepper offers a rounded spiciness balanced by the hint of sweetness from cocoa, cinnamon, and allspice. To retain the spices' aromas, I cook the meat over a lower heat than the usual crazy-high fire. It allows a burnished brown crust to form while maintaining a center that's evenly medium-rare throughout.

1 tablespoon pimentón (sweet smoked paprika)

1 tablespoon unsweetened cocoa powder

1 teaspoon ground cumin

½ teaspoon ground allspice

¼ teaspoon ground cinnamon

Pinch cayenne pepper

Kosher salt and freshly ground black pepper

1½ pounds hanger steak

PREPARE A CHARCOAL GRILL FOR DIRECT COOKing over medium heat with the top and bottom vents open. While the grill heats, let the steak stand at room temperature.

Stir the pimentón, cocoa powder, cumin, allspice, cinnamon, and cayenne in a small bowl until well-mixed. Sprinkle 1½ teaspoons salt all over the steak, then season with pepper. Rub the spice mixture all over the steak to evenly coat.

Put the steak on the grate over the medium-hot coals and cover. Grill until the bottom is browned and releases easily from the grate, 4 to 5 minutes. Flip the steak, cover, and cook until the other side is browned, 4 to 5 minutes more. I like my steak medium-rare. When I press it, it has the same resistance as when I press the skin between my thumb and index finger when I open my palm.

Transfer to a cutting board and let rest for 5 minutes. Slice against the grain and serve with any accumulated juices.

*Entrecot al Cabrales*

# RIBEYE STEAK WITH BLUE CHEESE SAUCE

### SERVES 4

Any time I see blue cheese on a menu, I order the dish, no matter what it is. It's among my favorite cheeses and is often turned into a sauce in Spain, especially in Asturias, where Cabrales is made. (If you can't find Cabrales, use another strong but smooth blue cheese, such as Roquefort.) To keep the cheese from overpowering all the other flavors, I enrich the sauce with shallots, sherry, and beef stock. The steak and cheese are the stars here and they make for a luxurious meal.

2 (1-pound) bone-in or (12-ounce) boneless rib-eye steaks (1½ inches thick)

1 tablespoon plus 1 teaspoon blended oil, divided

1 tablespoon minced shallot

¼ cup dry sherry wine

1 cup Beef Stock (page 113) or store-bought unsalted beef stock

3 ounces blue cheese, such as Cabrales, crumbled

1 cup heavy cream

Kosher salt and freshly ground black pepper

LET THE STEAKS STAND AT ROOM TEMPERATURE for at least 30 minutes and up to 1 hour before cooking.

Combine 1 teaspoon oil and the shallot in a large saucepan. Cook over medium-low heat, stirring often, until the shallot softens and is just translucent, about 2 minutes. Add the sherry, raise the heat to medium-high, and boil until reduced by half, about 3 minutes. Add the broth, bring to a boil, and boil until reduced by half, about 7 minutes. Reduce the heat to medium-low. Whisk in the blue cheese until melted and smooth. Continue whisking while adding the cream in a steady stream. Reduce the heat to low and simmer, stirring often, until the sauce becomes silky and thick enough to coat the back of a spoon, about 15 minutes.

While the sauce simmers, cook the steaks. Heat the remaining tablespoon oil in a large cast-iron pan over high heat until very hot and smoking. Very generously season the steaks with salt and pepper on both sides and place in the hot oil. Reduce the heat to medium-high and cook until the bottom is nicely browned, 5 to 6 minutes. If the steaks start to brown too quickly, reduce the heat to medium or even medium-low. You want the center to cook through to a perfect medium-rare with a nicely browned but not burnt crust. Flip the steaks and cook until the other sides are nicely browned, 4 to 5 minutes. I like my steak medium-rare. When I press it, it has the same resistance as when I press the skin between my thumb and index finger when I open my palm.

Transfer the steaks to a cutting board and let rest for 5 minutes. Slice against the grain and serve with the blue cheese sauce.

## Canelones de Carne

# MEAT-FILLED PASTA ROLLS WITH BÉCHAMEL AND MANCHEGO CHEESE

⚹

**SERVES 8 AS A MAIN DISH
OR 12 AS A SMALL PLATE**

Canelones come steaming out of Catalan kitchens throughout the holidays. They're often served the day after Christmas because they're a good way to use up leftover meat. Plus, whole casseroles filled with the meaty pasta rolls smothered in creamy sauce are great for feeding big families. It's just what you want on a chilly winter day. I prefer to stuff my canelones with freshly braised meat sauce, but the technique below can be used with any cooked meat you have on hand or even tuna. That's what I love about Spanish food. Basic formulas are infinitely adaptable.

The other thing I like is how easy it is to re-create authentic Spanish food in the U.S. The only specialty item for canelones is the dried pasta squares, but I found a readily available substitute. Barilla makes and sells flat no-bake lasagna sheets that taste just like the originals and are even easier to use since they don't require pre-boiling.

8 no-boil straight-edged lasagna noodles

3½ cups whole milk

6 tablespoons unsalted butter

½ cup all-purpose flour

¾ teaspoon freshly grated nutmeg

¾ teaspoon kosher salt

¼ teaspoon ground white pepper

3 to 4 cups Braised Meat and Chicken Liver Tomato Sauce (page 108)

6 ounces Manchego cheese, grated (1½ cups)

ARRANGE ONE OVEN RACK IN THE UPPER THIRD of the oven and one in the center and preheat to 375°F.

Place the lasagna noodles in a 9- by 13- by 2-inch baking dish; it's okay if they overlap. Pour boiling water over them and separate them to make sure they don't stick to one another. Let stand for 5 minutes. Use a flat spatula to carefully transfer each noodle to a cutting board without breaking, then cut each in half crosswise to form two squares. Empty the dish and wipe clean.

Pour the milk into a large measuring cup with a spout. Microwave on high until hot, about 3½ minutes. Meanwhile, melt the butter in a medium saucepan over low heat. Add the flour and raise the heat to medium. Cook, stirring continuously with a silicone spatula and scraping the bottom. Let the mixture bubble to cook the raw flour taste out of it, but don't let it brown, stirring the whole time so the flour doesn't burn. Take it to just before it begins to color so you know the flour's cooked out, about 5 minutes.

Reduce the heat to medium-low and add the milk, a little at a time, whisking continuously. It should be the consistency of a runny sauce, thick enough to coat the back of a spoon, but not stiff. This béchamel is thin because you want it to be saucy even after it bakes. Bring it to a boil and whisk for 1 minute. Remove from the heat and whisk in the nutmeg, salt, and pepper.

Spread 1½ cups béchamel in the bottom of the dish. Spoon 2 heaping tablespoons meat sauce in a line down the center of 1 pasta square, then tightly roll the noodle around the filling. The ends of the pasta should overlap by a scant ¼ inch. Place the filled canelone seam side down over the béchamel in the dish in one corner. Repeat with the remaining noodles and meat sauce and arrange the filled canelones side by side in the dish. You should have 2 rows of 8 canelones.

Dollop the remaining 1½ cups béchamel over the canelones and spread evenly over the

*(Continued)*

pasta. Be sure to cover the pasta entirely, all the way to the edges of the pan, to prevent the pasta from burning when you broil the cheese. At this point, the dish can be covered tightly with plastic wrap and refrigerated for up to 1 week. Uncover before proceeding.

When ready to bake, cover the dish tightly with foil and bake on the center rack until really hot throughout and bubbling, about 45 minutes. It'll take longer to cook if it's been refrigerated. Change the oven setting to broil. Uncover the casserole and sprinkle the cheese evenly on top.

Broil on the upper rack until the cheese is golden brown, about 5 minutes. Remove from the oven and let sit for 10 minutes before serving.

# BRAISED MEAT AND CHICKEN LIVER TOMATO SAUCE

### MAKES 6 CUPS

Growing up, I loved my mom's Bolognese sauce, especially her combination of beef, pork, bacon, and chicken liver. When I decided to create a canelone dish for Cúrate, I immediately thought of that sauce. Even though it's not Spanish, it has the soulful warmth common to canelone fillings. I started with ground meat, but quickly switched to big cuts so I could braise chunks and end up with a shredded meat sauce. Chicken livers and bacon take it over the top with their decadence and are balanced by sweet carrots and dry wine. Be sure to cook with a bottle you'd drink. Your sauce tastes more elegant with it and it's the perfect pairing for this dish.

This sauce is meant for the Canelones (page 107) but you can spoon it over a pile of Olive Oil Potato Puree (page 165) or any type of pasta, rice, or bread.

1 tablespoon blended oil

1 pound pork butt or shoulder, cut into 2-inch cubes

1 pound beef bottom round roast, cut into 2-inch chunks

5 slices bacon (5 ounces), cut into ½-inch strips crosswise

3 tablespoons unsalted butter, divided

1 large or 2 small yellow onions, very finely chopped (1¼ cups)

1½ large stalks celery, very finely chopped (¾ cup)

½ large carrot, peeled and very finely chopped (½ cup)

¼ cup tomato paste

½ cup dry white wine

1 quart Chicken Stock (page 136) or store-bought unsalted chicken broth

½ pound chicken livers, veins removed

Kosher salt and freshly ground black pepper

PREHEAT THE OVEN TO 350°F.

Get the oil ripping hot over high heat in a very large Dutch oven. You want it almost smoking. If it's not hot enough, the meat won't brown properly. You're going to brown the meat in batches because you're never going to be able to fit all of it in one pan. You want them to brown and not steam. We're developing flavor in this step. Add the pork to the hot oil in a single layer, spacing the pieces 2 inches apart. Reduce the heat to medium-high, and cook, turning when the bottom is golden brown, and lightly brown the other side, 2 to 4 minutes total. You're only browning 2 sides because you don't need to cook it all the way at this point. Transfer the pork to a plate. Spoon out excess oil; you want just enough to coat the bottom of the pan. Repeat with the remaining pork and beef, working in batches with the meat spaced 2 inches apart. You can mix the pork and beef.

Turn off the heat and add the bacon. Turn the heat to medium and cook the bacon, stirring occasionally, until golden brown and crisp. Add 2 tablespoons butter, the onions, celery, and carrot. Cook, stirring occasionally, until very tender and just starting to brown, about 8 minutes. Push the vegetables to one side and add the tomato paste to the other side of the pan. Cook alone on that side of the pan, stirring, until caramelized, about 2 minutes. Stir with everything else in the pan and cook, stirring, until the mixture changes from bright red to a dark orange, almost amber color, about 4 minutes. Add the wine, bring to a boil, and reduce, stirring frequently, until the liquid has almost all evaporated. Cook out all the wine to take out the flavor of the alcohol and to lessen the acidity.

Add all of the meat with its accumulated juices and the chicken stock. Stir well. The chicken stock should just cover all of the solids. Bring to a boil over high heat, then cover with a lid and transfer to the oven. Braise until the meat is really tender, about 3 hours.

Uncover and let cool slightly, then shred all of the meat in the pot with forks until finely shredded.

Melt the remaining tablespoon butter over medium-high heat in a large skillet. Add the chicken livers and sear until the bottoms are browned, then flip and cook until other side is browned and they're firm to the touch, 5 to 7 minutes. When you poke a liver, it should bounce back. Transfer to a cutting board. When cool enough to handle, finely mince as you would if you were putting them in giblet gravy.

Mix the chicken livers into the meat mixture. Add 2 teaspoons salt, and taste. Add more salt if you'd like and season to taste with pepper. Use the sauce immediately in Canelones (page 107) or cool completely before chilling. The sauce can be refrigerated in an airtight container for up to 1 week or frozen for up to 1 month.

MEAT AND POULTRY

*Rabo de Toro*

# BRAISED OXTAIL

SERVES 6 AS A MAIN DISH
OR 10 AS A SMALL PLATE

Córdoba, in the center of the Andalucía province, specializes in this hearty braise. Oxtails, a bargain cut of meat, need to cook long and slow, to the point where the meat is falling off the bone. When you touch it with a fork, it should flake apart immediately. If it doesn't, don't be tempted to remove it from the oven. The seasonings here are straightforward because the cut of meat is the star. There's a lot of bone, marrow, and collagen in oxtails, and they enrich the sauce with an incomparable beefiness. You'll want to spoon it over Olive Oil Potato Puree (page 165) or scoop it up with crusty bread. An aged reserva tempranillo from Rioja balances the richness well. If you're looking to explore the world of sherry, try an Oloroso. All you need to round out the meal is a crisp salad.

5 pounds oxtails

4 ounces bacon, cut into ½-inch strips

Kosher salt and freshly ground black pepper

¼ cup all-purpose flour, divided

4 carrots, peeled and cut into large chunks

2 celery stalks, cut into large chunks

1 large yellow onion, cut into large chunks

3 garlic cloves, smashed and peeled

1 tablespoon tomato paste

1 750-ml bottle dry red wine

1 rosemary sprig

4 thyme sprigs

2 fresh or dried bay leaves

4 whole cloves

2 cups Beef Stock (page 113) or store-bought unsalted beef broth

PREHEAT THE OVEN TO 325°F. LET THE OXTAILS stand at room temperature.

Cook the bacon in a large Dutch oven or a large, deep ovenproof pot with a tight-fitting lid over medium-high heat, stirring frequently, until the bacon is crispy and brown and the fat has rendered, about 7 minutes. Use a slotted spoon to transfer the bacon to paper towels to drain, leaving the fat in the Dutch oven.

Meanwhile, season the oxtails with 1½ teaspoons salt and ½ teaspoon pepper, then dust with the flour. Shake off the excess flour and reserve, along with any unused flour because it will be added to the pan later to help thicken the sauce. Add a single layer of the oxtails to the hot bacon fat, spacing the pieces apart. Sear, turning to brown evenly on all sides, about 5 minutes. Transfer to a plate. Repeat with the remaining oxtail in two or more batches. Keep an eye on the temperature of the bacon fat so you don't burn the residual flour that begins to gather in the pan. Lower the heat if needed.

Add the carrots, celery, onion, and garlic to the Dutch oven. Cook, stirring frequently, until the vegetables begin to caramelize, 6 to 8 minutes. Add the tomato paste and cook, stirring, until caramelized, about 2 minutes.

Add the remaining flour to the Dutch oven and stir to coat all the vegetables. Add the wine, rosemary, thyme, bay leaves, and cloves. Bring to a simmer, scraping the browned bits from the bottom of the pan. Nestle the oxtails in the vegetables and wine. Add the beef stock and bring to a simmer. Cover and transfer to the oven.

Bake until the meat is falling off the bones, flipping the oxtails about halfway through, 3½ to 4 hours.

Carefully transfer the oxtails to a large bowl. Strain the sauce in the pan through a sieve, then return to the Dutch oven. Discard the solids in the sieve. Bring the sauce to a simmer over medium heat. The sauce should have thickened during the cooking, but if not, you can reduce it by simmering it until it thickens slightly. Taste the sauce and add salt if you'd like.

Return the oxtails to the Dutch oven and carefully turn to thoroughly coat in the sauce. Serve hot. At this point, the entire dish can be refrigerated in an airtight container for up to 3 days. Reheat in a 325°F oven for 30 minutes when you want to serve it.

# BEEF STOCK

MAKES ABOUT 2½ QUARTS

| | |
|---|---|
| 6 pounds beef bones | ¼ cup tomato paste |
| 2 carrots, peeled and coarsely chopped | 1 cup dry red wine |
| | 3 parsley sprigs |
| 2 celery stalks, coarsely chopped | 3 thyme sprigs |
| 2 medium onions, coarsely chopped | 1 fresh or dried bay leaf |
| 8 garlic cloves, smashed and peeled | 4 black peppercorns |
| | 4 whole cloves |

PREHEAT THE OVEN TO 450°F.

Arrange the bones in a single layer in a roasting pan. Roast for 30 minutes. Turn the bones over and stir in the carrots, celery, onions, garlic, and tomato paste. Roast for 30 minutes more, stirring halfway through. You want the bones nice and golden brown and the vegetables to be on the verge of browning.

Transfer everything to a large stockpot. Add the wine to the hot roasting pan and stir and scrape up all the browned bits. Pour into the stockpot. Bring the mixture to a simmer, then add just enough cold water to cover the solids. Add the parsley, thyme, bay leaf, peppercorns, and cloves. Bring to a boil over high heat, then reduce the heat to maintain a simmer. Simmer for 8 hours, replenishing the water if it falls below the solids.

Strain through a fine-mesh sieve, pressing on the solids to extract as much liquid as possible. Carefully ladle as much fat as possible off the top. Refrigerate the stock until cold. Remove and discard the solid pieces of fat on top. The stock can be refrigerated for up to 3 days or frozen for up to 3 months.

*Pinchos Morunos*

# MARINATED LAMB SKEWERS

### SERVES 4 AS A MAIN DISH
### OR 8 AS A SMALL PLATE

The Moors crossed into Spain from North Africa centuries ago and their cultural influence remains strong today. You can see it in the architecture and taste it in the cuisine. When opening Cúrate, we wanted to create a dish in homage to Moorish culture. The concept of grilled meat sticks comes from all over Spain and North Africa. These skewers smother lamb in a generously spiced marinade that blends the seasonings from both sides of the Strait of Gibraltar.

You can make these with precut lamb cubes. If you're cutting the meat yourself, you'll need to purchase about 3 pounds of boneless lamb shoulder or leg. Once you trim off all the fat and silverskin, you'll end up with 2 pounds of meat to cut into cubes.

¼ cup packed fresh cilantro leaves

¼ cup packed fresh flat-leaf parsley leaves

3 garlic cloves

2 tablespoons fresh lemon juice

1 tablespoon plus 1 teaspoon garam masala

1 tablespoon plus 1 teaspoon dried thyme

2 tablespoons pimentón (sweet smoked paprika)

2 dried arbol chiles

3 fresh or dried bay leaves

1½ teaspoons black peppercorns

1 cup blended oil

Kosher salt

2 pounds boneless lamb shoulder or leg of lamb, cut into 1-inch cubes

Cucumber Onion Pickles (recipe follows)

COMBINE THE CILANTRO, PARSLEY, GARLIC, LEMON juice, garam masala, thyme, pimentón, chiles, bay leaves, peppercorns, oil, and 2 teaspoons salt in a blender and blend on high until smooth.

Pour the marinade over the lamb in a bowl and mix until all of the lamb pieces are evenly coated. Cover tightly with plastic wrap and refrigerate for 18 to 24 hours.

Two hours before you're ready to cook, soak 16 (6-inch-long) bamboo skewers in cold water. (You can skip this step if you're using metal skewers.)

When you're ready to cook, heat an outdoor grill, preferably charcoal, or indoor grill pan to high. Thread five or six lamb pieces on each skewer. Season each skewer on all sides with salt.

Grill the skewers, turning once, until medium, about 4 to 6 minutes total. The outside should be charred and the meat should have a little resistance if you press it. Serve immediately with the Cucumber Onion Pickles.

## CUCUMBER ONION PICKLES

### MAKES ABOUT 2 CUPS

Pickles aren't common in Spain, but they taste great with some Spanish dishes, like Pinchos Morunos. The sour crunch of this half-sour pickle simultaneously cuts through the richness of the lamb and accentuates the complexity of the spiced marinade.

½ sweet onion

1 English cucumber

½ cup granulated sugar

2 teaspoons kosher salt

¾ cup sherry vinegar

USING A MANDOLINE OR THE SLICING BLADE OF A food processor, slice the onion as thinly as possible and the cucumber into ¹⁄₁₆-inch slices. Transfer both to an airtight container.

Bring the sugar, salt, and ¾ cup water to a simmer in a small saucepan over medium heat, stirring occasionally, until the sugar and salt have dissolved. Remove from the heat, stir in the vinegar, and pour over the cucumber and onion. Cover tightly and refrigerate at least overnight and up to 1 week.

*Chuletas de Cordero*

# LAMB CHOPS WITH BLACK OLIVE AND ROSEMARY CRUMBLE

**SERVES 2 TO 4 AS A MAIN DISH
OR 6 TO 8 AS A SMALL PLATE**

Individual lamb rib chops can be enjoyed in a fraction of the time it takes to cook a whole rack with this simple weeknight preparation. Thin single rib chops sear quickly and can be divvied up among as few or as many people as you'd like. In addition to giving the meat a deep sear, I also keep the spirit of a lamb rack's crust by making a crunchy crumb sprinkle. When fried, olives become as crisp as the toasted bread crumbs while retaining their acidic brininess. Lamb is popular in the Ribera del Duero region, which produces the wine that would taste best with the rich meat.

**¼ cup minced pitted Kalamata olives**

**3 tablespoons plus ½ teaspoon extra-virgin olive oil, divided**

**¼ cup panko (Japanese bread crumbs)**

**2 teaspoons minced garlic**

**8 (1-inch-thick) single rib lamb chops**

**Kosher salt and freshly ground black pepper**

**2 teaspoons finely chopped fresh rosemary leaves**

**Zest of ½ orange**

IF THE OLIVES ARE VERY WET, SCATTER THEM between paper towels and press gently to remove excess moisture. Heat 2 tablespoons oil in a large skillet over medium heat until hot. Add the olives and cook, stirring often, until crisp but not burnt, 2 to 3 minutes. Add the panko and cook, stirring, until golden brown, about 1 minute. Push the olives and crumbs to one side of the pan and add ½ teaspoon oil and the garlic to the other side. Cook, stirring, until fragrant, about 15 seconds, then stir into the crumb mixture. Remove from the heat.

Sprinkle the chops on all sides with 1½ teaspoons salt, then season with pepper. Heat the remaining 1 tablespoon oil in a very large skillet over high heat until very hot. Add 4 chops and cook, turning once, until nicely browned, about 3 minutes per side. Turn each chop on its top side to sear the fat for 1 minute. Transfer to serving plates. Repeat with the remaining chops.

Let the chops rest for a few minutes while you stir the rosemary and orange zest into the crumb mixture. Sprinkle the crumble mixture on top and serve immediately.

# HAM- AND CHEESE- STUFFED FRIED PORK CHOPS

SERVES 4

These cheesy, crunchy pork chops are the most popular kid-friendly meal in Spain. They're usually thrown together with cheap, rubbery cheese, so I've decided to elevate it for discerning kids and all adults. I shave the cheese fresh from a block of Cordobés or Manchego and add piquillos to cut through the richness and bring some brightness in taste and appearance. Plus, vegetables.

I like the pork-on-pork action with the chops and ham, but the same technique can be applied to skinless, boneless chicken breasts, too.

PLACE EACH PORK CHOP BETWEEN LARGE SHEETS of plastic wrap and pound with a meat mallet, heavy skillet, or rolling pin until ⅛ inch thick. Season both sides of each chop with salt and pepper. Place 1½ slices ham on each chop in a single layer to cover the surface, then layer the cheese and piquillos on one half of each chop. Fold each chop in half like a book to enclose the cheese and piquillos.

Place the flour in a shallow dish, beat the egg in another, and spread the panko in a third. Carefully dredge all sides of the stuffed pork chops in the flour and shake off the excess. Then, coat in the beaten egg and dredge in the panko. Tap off any excess crumbs.

Add enough oil to a large skillet to come ¼ inch up the sides. Heat over medium-high heat until hot. A panko crumb should sizzle immediately when dropped in. Add 2 breaded chops and cook, turning once, until golden brown, about 3 minutes per side. Drain on paper towels and season lightly with salt. Repeat with the remaining pork chops and serve immediately.

**4 (¾-inch-thick) boneless pork loin chops**

**Kosher salt and freshly ground black pepper**

**6 deli-thin slices Black Forest ham**

**3 ounces Cordobés or Manchego cheese, shaved into paper-thin slices with a vegetable peeler**

**4 piquillo peppers, cut open**

**¼ cup all-purpose flour**

**1 large egg**

**1 cup panko (Japanese bread crumbs)**

**Canola oil, for frying**

*Costillas de Cerdo en Adobo*

# PORK SPARE RIBS IN ADOBO SAUCE

⟡

**SERVES 8 AS A MAIN DISH
OR 12 AS A SMALL PLATE**

Lomo en adobo, pork loin in adobo, is served throughout Spain. But I live in the American South, where barbecue ribs rule. More specifically, I'm in North Carolina, home to vinegary barbecue sauces, my favorite type. Given my upbringing in Carolina-style barbecue, my adobo finds a welcome balance of smoke, spice, sourness, and sweetness and is slathered on ribs. The instructions below call for the oven so that you can cook these year round. If you have a smoker and know how to use it, do. If you don't eat pork, but want to try the sauce, smear it all over chicken and roast or grill it.

¼ **cup pimentón (sweet smoked paprika)**

3 **tablespoon dried thyme**

1 **tablespoon plus 1½ teaspoons ground coriander**

1 **tablespoon ground cumin**

3 **garlic cloves, peeled**

½ **cup plus 1 tablespoon reserve sherry vinegar**

¼ **cup honey**

6 **piquillo peppers**

5 **tablespoons extra-virgin olive oil**

**Kosher salt**

2 **(3½-pound) racks St. Louis-style pork spare ribs**

**Freshly ground black pepper**

PREHEAT THE OVEN TO 250°F. LINE A HALF-SHEET pan with foil and fit with a wire rack.

Puree the pimentón, thyme, coriander, cumin, garlic, vinegar, honey, piquillos, oil, and 1 tablespoon salt in a blender until smooth, scraping the bowl if needed. Transfer one-third of the adobo sauce to an airtight container and reserve.

Sprinkle the ribs on all sides with 4 teaspoons salt and season with pepper. Rub the remaining adobo sauce all over the ribs and place side by side, meat sides up, on the rack in the pan.

Bake for 2 hours. Brush the reserved adobo sauce all over the ribs and arrange on the rack meat side up again. Place a sheet of parchment paper over the ribs, then cover with foil. Bake until the meat is very tender and pulls away from the ends of the bones, about 2 hours longer.

Remove the ribs from the oven, uncover, and carefully turn bone side up. Position a rack 6 inches from the broiler heat source and adjust the oven heat to broil.

When the broiler is hot, broil the ribs until brown and crackly, about 3 minutes. Carefully turn the ribs meat side up and broil until the sauce is caramelized and bubbling, about 3 minutes. Let cool slightly, then cut into ribs and serve.

(From top) Butifarra, Chorizo,
Blood Sausages with Rice

# HOMEMADE PORK SAUSAGES

MAKES ABOUT 12 SAUSAGES

Fresh Spanish sausages are hard to come by stateside. At the restaurant, we have wonderful Spanish sausage suppliers. At my local grocery stores, not so much. I'm not going to claim that making sausage from scratch is easy or fast. It's neither. But it is worthwhile because you can't taste them unless you travel to Spain or an authentic Spanish restaurant in America.

Butifarra, Catalonia's sausage staple, is a prime example of how something so simple can be so delicious. Just a hint of nutmeg takes it to that next level. In American grocery stores, unadulterated fresh pork sausages are hard to come by. They always have fennel or chile or bits of peppers or even apples. In Butifarra, pork's pure flavor comes through. So, be sure to buy quality pasture-raised meat. The same is true for chorizo, even though it's spiked with more aggressive seasonings. In American supermarkets, chorizo is usually sold in its cured form. Cooked as fresh links, they burst with smoky spiced juices and a heady hit of wine.

I love the snap of the casings on crisped sausages, but the meat mixture still tastes good if you want to skip the stuffing step. Simply form into patties or torpedoes and pan-fry until browned and cooked through. You'll still need a meat grinder to make the mix though. A food processor will leave you with too many chewy bits.

## BUTIFARRA

2 pounds boneless, skinless, fatless pork butt, cut into 1-inch chunks

8 ounces pork fat, cut into 1-inch chunks

2 tablespoons kosher salt

1 teaspoon freshly ground black pepper

¾ teaspoon freshly grated nutmeg

5 feet natural hog casings

SPREAD THE PORK BUTT AND FAT ON A HALF-sheet pan in a single layer and freeze until thoroughly chilled, but not completely frozen through, about 1 hour. At the same time, place the bowl, paddle attachment, and the meat grinding attachment's large die plate of a KitchenAid standing mixer in the freezer.

Right before grinding, fill a bowl slightly larger than the mixer bowl with ice and water. Place under the meat grinder attachment. Set up the meat grinder attachment with the chilled large die plate. Combine the salt, pepper, and nutmeg in a large bowl. Add the chilled pork and fat and toss until well-coated. Set the mixer bowl in the bowl of ice water.

Turn the mixer speed to medium-high and drop 4 to 5 pieces of pork mixed with several chunks of fat into the feed tube. Press through the grinder with the tool that comes with the grinder attachment; do not try to use any other plunger to push the meat through. Once all the meat is ground, remove the mixer bowl from the ice bath and fit into the mixer with the paddle attachment.

Add ½ cup ice-cold water and mix on medium speed for 30 seconds. Transfer to the refrigerator and chill until very cold.

Meanwhile, soak the casings in room temperature water for 20 minutes. You want the casings to feel soft. Run cold water through the softened casings to rinse out the insides.

If you have a sausage stuffer, set it up with the largest tube. If you can clamp the sausage stuffer to the table, that would be ideal. Otherwise, find someone to help you hold it in place. Wet the counter or cutting board in front of the stuffer so that the filled casings will slide and coil neatly without sticking.

*(Continued)*

Add the chilled sausage mixture to the stuffing chamber and press flat. Crank until the meat just comes to the end of the tube and stop. Run some cold water over the tube and spoon a small amount of water into the opening of the casings, then slowly slide the casings onto the sausage tube, using more water to lubricate if necessary. Feed all but 2 inches of the casings onto the tube. Tie a knot at the very end of the casings.

Start cranking! You want to crank steadily once you start. I use a nice steady motion and, at the same time, slightly pull on the casings as the meat fills it. You don't want to stop cranking because that will create air pockets.

Once all the meat is in the casings, you'll want to measure 6 inches for each link. Pinch the two spots where you want to create a link, pressing the sausage meat away from those points and gently toward the middle to create room in the casings for a twist. Twist that link away from you. Then pinch the spot for a second adjacent link, but do not twist it. Do the same for the third link, then twist it the same way you did the first. As you do so, the second link will naturally twist as well. Repeat until the whole thing is twisted into links.

If you don't have a sausage stuffer, you can use a pastry bag instead. This is a case in which you can't substitute a resealable plastic bag for a plastic pastry bag. You need the stiffness and shape of a proper pastry bag. You'll also need someone to help you. Cut twelve 2-inch lengths of kitchen string. Snip a ½-inch hole at the end of the bag and rinse the inside of the bag with cold water. Rinse the inside of the casings with cold water. Stuff enough of the sausage filling into the bag to come two-thirds of the way up the sides. Slide the open end of the casing over the end of the bag and tie a piece of kitcnen string 7 inches from the end. Squeeze the mixture into the casing, in one continuous motion if possible, into a 6-inch length. Slide the casing off the bag and squeeze the casing around the filling into an even sausage shape. Tie the other end shut and snip the sausage off the remaining casing. Repeat with the remaining casing and filling, rewetting or replacing the piping bag as needed.

Prick the casings of the finished sausages with a clean needle to remove any air pockets. Place the links on a half-sheet pan in a single layer and refrigerate uncovered until very dry, about 2 hours. The sausages will form a pellicle, which is a taut, thin skin that ensures a nice crisp exterior after cooking. At this point, you can cut in between the links to separate. The sausages can be refrigerated in airtight resealable plastic bags for up to 3 days or frozen for up to 1 month. If frozen, thaw overnight in the refrigerator before cooking.

To grill the sausage, cook over low indirect heat, turning occasionally, until lightly browned and very hot in the center, about 25 minutes. To sauté the sausages, cook in a cast-iron skillet over medium-low heat, turning once, until browned and very hot in the center, about 20 minutes.

## CHORIZO

INCREASE THE BLACK PEPPER TO 2 TEASPOONS. Substitute 3 tablespoons hot pimentón (hot smoked paprika), 2 tablespoons pimentón (sweet smoked paprika), and 3 tablespoons minced garlic for the nutmeg. Substitute ½ cup very cold dry white wine for the water. Proceed as above.

*Morcilla de Burgos*

# BLOOD SAUSAGES
## WITH RICE

MAKES ABOUT 20 SAUSAGES

Blood sausage is one of my favorite Spanish delicacies, especially the rice-studded variety known as burgos. The tender rice grains break up the tight texture and cut through the meatiness. The most difficult part of this dish is tracking down fresh pork blood, which has a rounded taste that's far less tannic than beef blood. The sausage mix itself is actually much easier to stuff than Pork Sausages (page 125). Once you make a full batch, you can keep the links in your freezer for a 20-minute meal.

½ cup bomba, calasparra, or Arborio rice

1 tablespoon plus 2½ teaspoons kosher salt

8 ounces pork fat back, cut into ¼-inch cubes

1 tablespoon canola oil, plus more for cooking

1 cup finely chopped onion

1 large egg yolk

¼ cup heavy cream

1 tablespoon pimentón (sweet smoked paprika)

1 tablespoon hot pimentón (hot smoked paprika)

½ teaspoon ground cinnamon

½ teaspoon ground cloves

½ teaspoon freshly grated nutmeg

½ teaspoon freshly ground black pepper

8 ounces store-bought pork blood, strained (1 cup)

10 feet natural hog casings, rinsed

1 2-liter plastic soda bottle, bottom cut off

Extra-virgin olive oil, for serving

Baguette toast points, for serving

BRING A LARGE SAUCEPAN OF WATER TO A BOIL. Stir in the rice and 1 tablespoon salt. Boil the rice like pasta until cooked through and tender, about 12 minutes. Drain, rinse with cold running water until cold, then drain well. Spread on a half-sheet pan and refrigerate until cool.

Bring a medium saucepan of water to a boil. Add the pork fat and reduce the heat to maintain a steady simmer for 20 minutes. Meanwhile, heat the canola oil in a large skillet over medium heat. Add the onion and cook, stirring occasionally, until translucent, about 10 minutes. Transfer to a large bowl. Drain the pork fat and add to the onion. Refrigerate until cold.

Whisk the egg yolk, cream, pimentón and hot pimentón, cinnamon, cloves, nutmeg, pepper, and remaining 2½ teaspoons salt in a large bowl. Stir in the pork blood until well combined, then stir in the chilled rice, onion, and pork fat until evenly distributed. Refrigerate until cold.

Meanwhile, soak the casings in room temperature water for 20 minutes. You want the casings to feel soft. Run cold water through the softened casings to rinse out the insides.

Set up an area to fill the casings. Wet a half-sheet pan to create a slick surface and put the casings on it. Pull one end of the casings over the mouth of the bottle, leaving the rest of the casings on the wet pan. With kitchen string, tie the casings around the bottle opening tightly and tie the opposite end shut. Hold the casing against the bottle shut with one hand while ladling the blood sausage mixture into the wide-open end of the bottle. Ladle in enough to come three-quarters of the way up the sides. Slowly release your fingers around the other end to let the mixture slowly flow through without creating air bubbles. If the solids have trouble getting through the opening, push them through with the handle of a wooden spoon. Repeat with the remaining sausage mixture until the casings are completely full. Tie the end closest to the bottle shut and snip off the part tied to the bottle. Gently massage the mixture to evenly distribute the solids. Starting from one end, tie into 6-inch links with kitchen string using double knots. Don't make the links too taut and firm or they'll burst when cooking. When you press a link, it should have the wobbly softness of a poached egg. Once all the links are made, tie the two ends together to create a ring.

Bring a large pot of water to 170°F. Carefully lower the sausage ring into the pot and poach for 20 minutes, adjusting the heat as needed to maintain a constant 170°F.

To check for doneness, carefully pull a sausage up over the edge of the pot with the end of a wooden spoon lifting between links and prick a link with a needle. Brown, not red, liquid should ooze out.

Carefully transfer to a half-sheet pan in a single layer and cool to room temperature. Transfer to the refrigerator and chill until cold and the casings are dry, about 2 hours. The sausages can be refrigerated in an airtight container for up to 3 days or frozen for up to 1 month.

When ready to serve, cook in a lightly oiled pan over medium-low heat until crisp on the outside and very hot inside, about 15 minutes. Transfer to a cutting board and slice into rounds. Return to the pan and cook until both sides are well-seared. Transfer to a serving plate, drizzle with olive oil, and spear with toothpicks. Serve with toast points.

MEAT AND POULTRY

**BLOOD SAUSAGES WITH RICE**

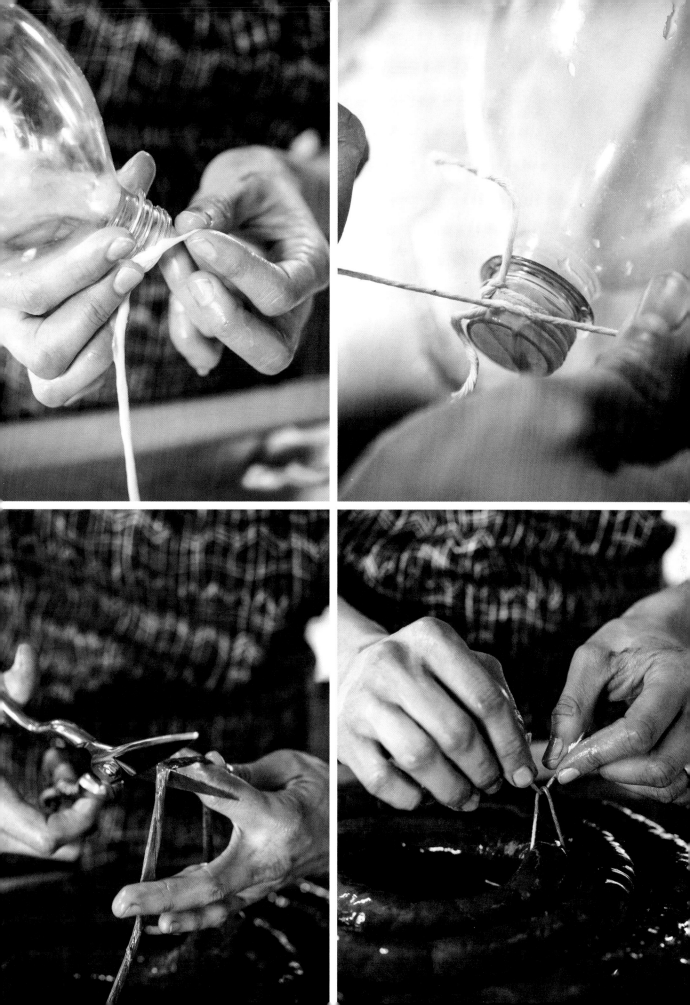

*Conejo en Salmorejo*

# BRAISED RABBIT IN SALMOREJO SAUCE

SERVES 4

For years, I wanted to collaborate with a local North Carolina farm that raises rabbits. They treat the animals with such respect that I wanted to support them by becoming a significant and steady buyer, so I began researching Spanish rabbit dishes. I found a winner from the Canary Islands, which are in the Atlantic off the Southwestern coast of Spain. Rabbit dishes abound there. To keep the lean meat moist, I brine it to make it extra succulent and braise it until it's fall-off-the-bone tender. Dark meat chicken works here, too, but doesn't taste quite as complex. Eat this with a red wine from the Canary Islands. Their grapes grow in volcanic soils, yielding wines with a light body but a kind of funky bite.

### BRINE

¼ cup kosher salt

¼ cup packed light brown sugar

2 fresh or dried bay leaves

2 garlic cloves, smashed and peeled

10 black peppercorns

1 whole (3-pound) rabbit or 2½ pounds bone-in, skin-on chicken thighs

### BRAISE

5 garlic cloves

1½ teaspoons fresh oregano leaves

1 teaspoon fresh thyme leaves

2 dried Nora chiles or 1 small New Mexico chile, stemmed and seeded

1 fresh or dried bay leaf

2 teaspoons pimentón (sweet smoked paprika)

(BRAISE continued)

½ teaspoon ground cumin

2 tablespoons white wine vinegar

1½ cups dry white wine, preferably Albariño

2 tablespoons blended oil

TO MAKE THE BRINE, COMBINE THE SALT, SUGAR, bay leaves, garlic, and peppercorns in a small saucepan and add 1 cup water. Bring to a boil, stirring to dissolve the salt and sugar. Remove from the heat and stir in 2 cups water to cool. Transfer to a large bowl and refrigerate until cold.

Cut the rabbit into 6 pieces: 2 hind legs, 2 front legs, and back with loin attached then split in half crosswise to form 2 pieces. Submerge in the brine, cover tightly with plastic wrap, and refrigerate for at least 6 hours and up to 24 hours. Remove from the brine and pat dry.

To make the braise, preheat the oven to 350°F.

Puree the garlic, oregano, thyme, chiles, bay leaf, pimentón, cumin, vinegar, and 1½ cups water in a blender until smooth. With the machine running, add the wine in a steady stream.

Heat the oil in a large Dutch oven or large, deep saucepot over medium-high heat. Add half of the rabbit pieces and sear, turning once, until golden brown, 2 to 3 minutes per side. Transfer to a plate and repeat with the remaining rabbit.

Drain excess oil from the Dutch oven, then add the wine mixture and the rabbit with its accumulated juices. If the liquid doesn't cover the rabbit, add enough water so that the meat is barely covered. Bring to a boil, cover, and transfer to the oven.

Braise in the oven until the meat is very tender and almost falling off the bone, about 1½ hours.

Carefully transfer the rabbit pieces to a platter. Bring the cooking liquid to a boil on the stovetop and reduce until thickened slightly. Pour the sauce over the rabbit and serve with crusty bread, the potatoes from the Patatas Bravas (page 169) or Olive Oil Potato Puree (page 165).

# CHICKEN STOCK

MAKES ABOUT 13½ CUPS STOCK

From-scratch chicken stock has a purer, more intense chicken and vegetable flavor than canned but isn't salty. Leaving stock unsalted gives you the flexibility of seasoning each dish to taste. And I scrub—not peel—the carrots. The peel doesn't taste bad, so there's no point in not using it.

To keep chicken stock on hand, freeze in stackable airtight pint or quart containers.

**2 pounds chicken neck, wings, and/or bones**

**2 large carrots, coarsely chopped**

**2 celery stalks, coarsely chopped**

**2 large yellow onions, coarsely chopped**

**1 head garlic, cut in half crosswise, extra skins removed**

**6 sprigs thyme**

**2 dried bay leaves**

**1 teaspoon black peppercorns**

COMBINE ALL OF THE INGREDIENTS IN A LARGE stockpot. Add 12 cups cold water, then add more if needed to just cover the solids. Bring to a boil over high heat. Reduce the heat to maintain a low simmer; it should be bubbling only occasionally. Simmer for 1½ hours. If the water level ever goes under the chicken, be sure to add more cold water. Bring it up to a boil again, then bring it back down.

Strain the stock through a fine-mesh sieve or colander into another pot or container.

Cover the stock tightly and refrigerate for up to 7 days or freeze for up to 3 months. To freeze the stock in smaller batches, cool the stock quickly in a large shallow dish in the fridge, then divide among smaller airtight containers and freeze.

To use frozen stock, zap the container in the microwave or immerse in a bowl of hot water for 30 seconds to pop the frozen stock out of the container. Put the block in a saucepan over super-low heat until melted. You don't want to boil it because you don't want it to evaporate.

*El Pollo de Pepa*

# PEPA'S BEER-BRAISED CHICKEN

### SERVES 4

This was Félix's favorite dish by his mother while growing up, so he asked that I learn to make it once we decided to settle in America. It's the ideal dish for Asheville, which is a beer mecca. Any lighter pale ale or lager or Kölsch-style beer is nice. Since you need only a can and a half, make sure you choose something you'd like to drink. If you're not into craft beer or don't happen to have any at home when you're craving braised chicken, use dry white wine or sherry instead.

One of my favorite parts about this dish is that it can be made ahead of time. It's really easy to put together, but it's nice to be able to simply reheat it on busy weeknights or just before guests arrive on weekends. If you decide to add the potatoes, this becomes a one-pot meal. Otherwise, serve it with a crusty whole-grain or sourdough loaf.

1 whole (3¾-pound) chicken

Kosher salt and freshly ground black pepper

¼ cup blended oil, plus more if needed

1 medium yellow onion, thinly sliced

4 garlic cloves, peeled and thinly sliced

2 cups beer, dry white wine, or dry sherry wine

1 tablespoon minced fresh flat-leaf parsley

Patatas Bravas (page 169) potatoes only, optional

**B**REAK DOWN THE CHICKEN BY CUTTING IT INTO 10 pieces: 2 wings (wing tips removed), 2 thighs, 2 drumsticks, and 4 breast pieces (each breast half cut in half crosswise). You can ask your butcher to do this for you. Season the chicken pieces on all sides with 2 teaspoons salt and ½ teaspoon pepper.

Heat the oil in a large, deep skillet over high heat until very hot. The oil should coat the bottom of the pan to a depth of ⅛ inch; add more if needed. Add half of the chicken and cook, turning once, until golden brown on both sides, 4 to 6 minutes. Transfer to a plate. Repeat with the remaining chicken.

Reduce the heat to medium and add the onion and garlic. Cook, stirring frequently, until soft, about 5 minutes. Nestle all of the chicken with its juices in the pan in a single snug layer. Pour in the beer, raise the heat to high, and bring to a simmer. Reduce the heat to medium-low and move the chicken pieces a little bit so they nestle in the sauce a little better.

Cover and cook until the breast pieces just lose their pinkness. Start checking after 10 minutes, but they may take up to 20 minutes, depending on how thick and large they are. When you pull a breast piece out, you want it to be just cooked. Transfer the breast pieces to a plate. Cover again and continue to simmer the rest of the chicken until very tender. Start checking after 10 minutes, but they may take up to 25 minutes more. When you poke them with a fork, their meat should pull away from the bone easily.

Uncover the skillet, raise the heat to high, and boil the sauce until the acidity of the alcohol has cooked off and the sauce has thickened slightly, 3 to 5 minutes. Put the chicken breast pieces and any accumulated juices back in the pan and turn to coat in the sauce and to warm them. Toss in the minced parsley and add the potatoes if you'd like. If you are adding the potatoes, let them rest for a couple of minutes to soak up some of the sauce before serving.

*Pollo al Ast*

# LEMON-ROSEMARY ROAST CHICKEN WITH POTATOES AND APPLES

SERVES 4 TO 6

Throughout Spain, shops dedicated to rotisserie chickens have the birds spinning all day, dripping their juices onto trays of roasted potatoes below. I've tried to re-create the effect in the oven, baking the chicken breast side down at a low temperature, then turning it right side up to brown the skin without overcooking the meat. Because the chicken roasts on a rack, its skin crisps all around and its drippings soak into the potatoes and apples—my autumnal add-in.

| | |
|---|---|
| 1 whole (4-pound) chicken | 1 lemon, halved, divided |
| Kosher salt and freshly ground black pepper | 2 large sweet-tart apples (12 ounces), such as Honeycrisp |
| Extra-virgin olive oil | 2 large Yukon gold potatoes (1 pound) |
| | 10 rosemary sprigs |

PREHEAT THE OVEN TO 300°F.

Pat the chicken dry and place it in a bowl. Sprinkle it inside and out with 1 tablespoon salt, then season the skin with pepper. Rub just enough oil to coat the skin. Squeeze 2 tablespoons juice from a lemon half and sprinkle all over the chicken. Let stand while you prepare the apples and potatoes.

Cut the apples into eighths to create 1-inch-thick wedges; discard the core. Scrub the potatoes and cut into 1-inch chunks. Toss the apples and potatoes with 2 teaspoons oil and 1½ teaspoons salt on a half-sheet pan. Spread in a single layer, leaving a space in the center for the chicken, and top with 4 rosemary sprigs. Place a rack over the mixture.

Stuff the chicken with the remaining lemon half and 6 rosemary sprigs. Truss tightly, then place on the rack breast side down over the empty space reserved for it. Pour the juices from the bowl all over the chicken.

Roast until an instant-read thermometer inserted into the thickest part of the thigh registers 125°F, about 35 minutes. If your oven doesn't heat evenly, be sure to rotate the pan halfway through. Remove the pan from the oven and raise the oven temperature to 450°F.

When the oven reaches 450°F, carefully turn the chicken breast side up. Roast until golden brown and an instant-read thermometer inserted into the breast registers 150°F, about 25 minutes. If the chicken isn't as browned as you'd like, you can change the oven setting to broil, turning the pan to evenly color.

Transfer the chicken to a cutting board and let rest for 5 minutes. Transfer the potatoes and apples to a serving platter. Carve the chicken and serve.

*Escalopines de Pollo con Setas*

# CHICKEN BREASTS WITH SHERRIED MUSHROOMS

SERVES 4

From start to finish, this weeknight meal takes about 30 minutes. But that's enough time for the mushrooms to deepen their natural flavor with a sear in olive oil, then a simmer in sherry. This is a typical quick dish found in homes throughout Spain, but it originated in Jerez, where sherry is made. This simple meal can be made with boneless pork loin chops instead of chicken as well.

2 (8-ounce) skinless, boneless chicken breast halves

Kosher salt and freshly ground black pepper

3 tablespoons plus 2 teaspoons extra-virgin olive oil, divided

1 pound mushrooms, preferably a mix of wild mushrooms, cut into bite-size pieces

4 garlic cloves, peeled and thinly sliced

½ cup dry sherry wine

1 fresh or dried bay leaf

1 thyme sprig

½ cup Chicken Stock (page 136) or store-bought unsalted chicken stock

½ cup heavy cream

CUT THE CHICKEN BREAST HALVES THROUGH their equators to create thinner cutlets. You should now have 4 pieces that are the same shape as the original, but ½- to ¾-inch thick. Sprinkle 1 teaspoon salt all over the chicken, then season with pepper.

Heat 1 tablespoon oil in a large cast-iron skillet over high heat until smoking hot. Add 2 chicken pieces and sear, turning once, until golden brown, about 2 minutes. Transfer to a plate. Repeat with another tablespoon oil and the remaining chicken.

Add another tablespoon oil, then add the mushrooms. Stir well, then spread in an even layer. Cook, stirring once or twice, until the mushrooms are nicely browned and tender, about 7 minutes. Push them to one side of the pan. Reduce the heat to medium and add the remaining 2 teaspoons oil to the other side of the skillet. Add the garlic and cook, stirring, until just golden, about 1 minute. Stir into the mushrooms, then add the sherry, bay leaf, and thyme. Bring to a boil, then simmer until the liquid has reduced by half, about 2 minutes.

Add the chicken stock, bring to a boil, then simmer until reduced by half, about 6 minutes. Add the cream and ½ teaspoon salt. Simmer, stirring occasionally, until thickened, about 5 minutes.

Return the chicken to the skillet and turn to coat with the sauce and heat through. Simmer until the chicken just loses its pinkness throughout, about 2 minutes. Serve immediately.

*Codorniz en Escabeche*

# QUAIL IN ESCABECHE

⟁

SERVES 4 WITH QUAIL
OR 8 WITH POUSSINS

Throughout Spain, this quail dish is usually served cold or room temperature. The birds soak in the vinegary sauce for up to a week, taking on an intense tartness. I don't like eating generously sauced poultry at room temperature, so I decided to serve this hot. The key is to simmer the cooking liquid to the point when the acid has burned off and the natural sugars in the vinegar start to caramelize. That results in a silky sauce with a welcome tang.

4 whole (4-ounce) quails, or 2 (1¼-pound) poussins

1 cup pearl onions

Kosher salt and freshly ground black pepper

¼ cup plus 3 tablespoons extra-virgin olive oil

8 garlic cloves, smashed and peeled

1 carrot, peeled and cut into ¼-inch-thick rounds (½ cup)

2 scallions, thinly sliced

1 fresh or dried bay leaf

2 strips orange zest, removed with a vegetable peeler

1 dried guindilla or arbol chile

1 cup dry sherry wine

1 cup sherry vinegar

IF YOU'RE USING BONE-IN QUAIL OR THE POUSSINS, start by splitting them in half. Using kitchen shears, cut along one side of the backbone, then the other, and discard the spine. Cut along one side of the breast bone, top to bottom, to split the birds in half. One side of each bird will be slightly larger since it has the breastbone.

To peel the pearl onions, fill a medium bowl with ice and water and bring a medium saucepan of water to a boil. Use a sharp paring knife to slit an "X" opposite the root ends of the pearl onions. Drop into the boiling water and boil for 45 seconds. Drain and immediately transfer to the ice water. When cool, slip off the outer papery layers of the onions. Trim the very end of the roots.

Sprinkle 1 teaspoon salt all over the quail (or 1½ teaspoons for the poussins). Season with pepper. Heat 1 tablespoon oil in a large Dutch oven over high heat until very hot. Add half the poultry and cook, turning once, until nicely seared, 2 to 3 minutes per side. Transfer to a plate and repeat with another tablespoon oil and the remaining birds.

Add another tablespoon oil, reduce the heat to medium-low, and add the garlic. Stir just until golden, about 15 seconds, then add the carrot. Cook, stirring often, until golden and starting to caramelize, 3 to 4 minutes. Add the pearl onions and cook, stirring often, until starting to turn golden brown, about 2 minutes. Add the scallions and stir for 30 seconds, then stir in the bay leaf, orange zest, and chile. Stir just until fragrant, then add the sherry. Bring to a boil, stirring and scraping up the browned bits. Add the vinegar, remaining ¼ cup oil, and 1 cup water. Bring to a boil, then simmer until reduced by half. Stir in ½ teaspoon salt.

Add the birds with any accumulated juices and nestle into the mixture. Simmer, turning the pieces occasionally, until the meat is cooked through, 5 to 7 minutes. When you press the meat with your fingertip, it should feel firm and not at all squishy. Transfer the birds to a serving platter. Taste the sauce. It should now be reduced and bubbling thickly like lava and the vinegar should taste a bit sweet. If not, simmer it longer. Spoon all over the poultry and serve hot.

# VEGETABLES

*Espárragos Blancos con Mayonesa*

# WHITE ASPARAGUS WITH AN AIRY MAYONNAISE

### SERVES 8 AS A SMALL PLATE

White asparagus in cans or jars is highly prized in Spain, particularly spears from the Navarra region. Those spears even receive a protected Denomination of Origin (D.O.) label. This is one of those cases in which fresh is not better because you'll be hard pressed to find fresh white asparagus as tasty as jarred unless you live in Navarra. The most popular way to enjoy this delicacy is with a side of mayonnaise. At the restaurant, I pipe mayonnaise out of a siphon to turn it into an airy sauce. I've created the technique in this recipe for a similar effect without the use of a siphon. To bring freshness to the jarred vegetables, I drizzle them with a bright lemon vinaigrette and sprinkle them with torn tarragon leaves.

## ASPARAGUS AND LEMON VINAIGRETTE

1 lemon

¼ teaspoon minced shallot

⅛ teaspoon kosher salt

2 tablespoons extra-virgin olive oil

Freshly ground black pepper

1 (16-ounce) can white asparagus, preferably from Navarra, drained

2 sprigs tarragon, leaves picked

## AIRY MAYONNAISE

1 large egg, room temperature

1 large egg yolk, room temperature

1½ teaspoons sherry vinegar

1 teaspoon Dijon mustard

¾ teaspoon kosher salt

½ cup blended oil

TO MAKE THE ASPARAGUS AND LEMON VINAI-grette, zest one-quarter of the lemon into a small bowl, then squeeze in 1½ teaspoons juice. Reserve the remaining lemon. Whisk in the shallot and salt. Slowly pour in the oil in a steady stream while whisking vigorously. Season to taste with pepper.

Arrange the asparagus on a serving platter and drizzle with the lemon vinaigrette. Zest the remaining lemon on top, then sprinkle with the tarragon leaves.

To make the airy mayonnaise, whip the egg and egg yolk with the whisk attachment of an electric mixer on medium-high speed until super light, foamy, and almost quadrupled in volume, about 5 minutes. Add the vinegar, mustard, and salt and whip for 10 seconds just to combine. Reduce the speed to medium. With the machine running, slowly pour in the oil in a steady stream.

Immediately spoon the airy mayonnaise on top of the asparagus and serve right away.

*Espárragos Verdes con Romesco*

# GRILLED ASPARAGUS WITH ROMESCO

SERVES 8 AS A SMALL PLATE

All asparagus season long, I keep bunches in the fridge. I stand them upright in a bowl of water so that they stay snappy until I'm ready to cook them. They're delicious simply grilled or roasted and served with romesco. Romesco can be prepared ahead of time, but should be served at room temperature.

*Romesco*

## ROASTED TOMATO, ONION, AND NUT SAUCE

MAKES ABOUT 2½ CUPS

There's no one version of this iconic Spanish sauce, just essential components. It's sweet with tomatoes, onion, and garlic, juicy with nuts and olive oil, thick with bread, tangy with vinegar, and smoky with pimentón. Proportions vary from cook to cook, and this is the mix I've landed on for its balance of sweet, sour, and smoky. It's great over any meat or vegetable, grilled in the summer or roasted in the winter.

One 6-inch piece baguette, crusts trimmed, bread cut into ½-inch cubes (1 cup)

1 tablespoon plus 1 teaspoon sherry vinegar

⅓ cup skin-on raw almonds

⅓ cup skin-on raw hazelnuts

1¼ pounds tomatoes (about 2 medium)

1½ teaspoons blended oil

1 small yellow onion, peeled and halved

2 heads garlic

½ cup extra-virgin olive oil

½ teaspoon pimentón (smoked sweet paprika)

Kosher salt

PREHEAT THE OVEN TO 400°F. IF YOUR BREAD isn't stale and dry, toast cubes on a half-sheet pan in the oven. You don't want any color, but you do want it to dry out. Place the bread cubes in a small bowl. Drizzle with the vinegar.

Spread the almonds and hazelnuts in a single layer on a half-sheet pan and bake until dark golden brown, about 12 minutes. Raise the oven temperature to 425°F.

Meanwhile, line another half-sheet pan with foil. Core the tomatoes, then mark an "X" on the other ends with the tip of a sharp knife. Rub 1 teaspoon oil all over the tomatoes and the onion on the prepared pan. Put the onion halves cut side down on another sheet of foil and wrap well. Put on the prepared pan, next to the tomatoes. Cut off the tops of the garlic heads to expose the cloves; discard the tops. Drizzle the remaining ½ teaspoon oil on the cut side. Place the garlic cut side down on a sheet of foil and wrap tightly. Place next to the onion.

Roast until the tomatoes are a darker shade of brown and their skins are wrinkly and peeled back from the cuts, about 35 minutes. Transfer them to a bowl. Return the pan to the oven. Continue roasting until the onion and garlic are tender and caramelized on the bottoms, about 15 minutes more. Let stand to cool.

When the tomatoes are cool enough to handle, peel them and discard the peel. Hold one over a bowl and gently squeeze out any excess liquid. Reserve the tomato juices in the bowl and

*(Continued)*

transfer the flesh to a food processor. Repeat with the remaining tomatoes. Squeeze the garlic out of their skins into the food processor. Add the onion, almonds, hazelnuts, soaked bread, olive oil, and smoked pimentón. Pulse until well combined, but still a little chunky. You want bits of nut present. If the mixture is too thick, pulse in a little of the reserved tomato juice.

Transfer to a bowl and season with 1 teaspoon salt. Taste and add more salt if you'd like. The romesco can be refrigerated in an airtight container for up to 1 week. Bring to room temperature before serving.

*Espárragos a la Brasa*

## GRILLED ASPARAGUS

| | |
|---|---|
| 1 bunch asparagus (1 pound) | Kosher salt |
| 1 tablespoon extra-virgin olive oil | 1 cup Romesco (page 148) at room temperature |

**P**REHEAT THE OVEN TO 425°F OR HEAT AN OUTdoor grill to high.

Snap off the ends of the asparagus where they naturally break, then trim the ends for even edges.

Toss the asparagus with the oil on a half-sheet pan until evenly coated, then sprinkle with ¼ teaspoon salt.

Roast or grill, turning once or twice, until crisp-tender, about 10 minutes. Taste and season with more salt if you'd like. Serve immediately with the Romesco.

*Escalivada*

# ROASTED EGGPLANT, ONION, AND PEPPERS WITH ROASTED VEGETABLE VINAIGRETTE

⊼

SERVES 4 AS A LIGHT ENTREE
OR 8 TO 12 AS A SMALL PLATE

Escalivada appears on tables all over Catalonia. Roasted onion, eggplant, and peppers come in all forms—as giant halves, big chunks, and fine dices—but I prefer them in thin strips. The slender shape allows them to readily soak up the vinaigrette made with their cooking juices. The dressed vegetables are a versatile side dish and taste, especially good with grilled meat. I like to top them with crumbled blue cheese, anchovies, or both. If you do that, you're almost at lunch. Throw some Pan con Tomate (page 22) at it and you've got a full meal. Arrange the mix on toast points and you're now armed with an elegant hors d'oeuvre.

| | |
|---|---|
| 1 medium yellow onion | 1½ teaspoons sherry vinegar |
| 3 tablespoons blended or canola oil, divided | Kosher salt |
| 1 medium eggplant | 1 tablespoon extra-virgin olive oil |
| 3 red bell peppers | |

**P**REHEAT THE OVEN TO 450°F. LINE A HALF-SHEET pan with foil.

Cut the onion in half through the root end and rub 1 tablespoon blended oil all over the onion. Place on the prepared pan, cut sides down. Rub the eggplant and peppers with the remaining 2 tablespoons blended oil and place on the pan alongside the onion.

Roast for 30 minutes and turn over the vegetables. Roast for 30 minutes more and turn the eggplant and peppers, then wrap the onion halves in foil to finish cooking them without letting the cut sides get too black. Roast until the peppers and eggplant are very black and blistery looking, 15 to 30 minutes more.

Carefully transfer the vegetables with their juices to a large bowl and immediately cover with plastic wrap. When the vegetables are cool enough to handle, remove the skins, stems, and seeds from the peppers. Transfer the peppers to a large cutting board. Remove the skin and stem from the eggplant and transfer the flesh to the board. Remove the skin and two to three tough outer layers from the onion and transfer the onion to the board.

Spoon 2 tablespoons of the accumulated juices from the vegetable bowl into a smaller bowl, leaving behind any solids or black bits. Whisk the vinegar and ¼ teaspoon salt into the juices, then whisk in the olive oil.

Cut the peppers, eggplant, and onion into ⅛-inch slices. Arrange them on a serving platter in sections, as if you're putting together a striped flag of eggplant, pepper, and onion. Sprinkle the cut vegetables with 1 teaspoon salt.

Whisk the vinaigrette again and pour over the vegetables. Cover with plastic wrap and refrigerate until ready to serve, at least an hour and up to a day.

*Pisto Manchego*

# STEWED PEPPERS, EGGPLANT, TOMATO, AND ONIONS

⌁

MAKES ABOUT 5 CUPS;
SERVES 8 AS A SMALL PLATE

1 large tomato (8½ ounces), cut in half crosswise

¼ cup blended oil

2 green bell peppers, stemmed, seeded, and cut into ½-inch dice (3 cups)

2 red bell peppers, stemmed, seeded, and cut into ½-inch dice (3 cups)

2 small yellow onions, cut into ½-inch dice (1½ cups)

1 packed tablespoon minced garlic (from about 4 large cloves)

1 large (1¼ pound) eggplant, peeled and cut into ½-inch dice

⅓ cup tomato paste

2 sprigs thyme

1 rosemary sprig

Kosher salt and freshly ground black pepper

If you think this sounds like ratatouille, you're right. Or, for that matter, caponata. Italy, France, and Spain share very similar Mediterranean dishes. The differences among the countries' versions stem from regional ingredients and cultural traditions. Some may argue over whose recipe appeared first, but I think what matters more is how it tastes now. I tossed in some thyme and rosemary, as I think those herbs lend a lovely aroma.

This stew originated in La Mancha, which is one of the largest wine regions in the world. Vineyards from that region produce beautiful wines, which would taste great with this dish.

Pisto Manchego morphs easily from appetizer to side dish to main dish. You may make a big batch and serve some on toast at the start of a meal. The next night, it might nestle next to roast chicken (see page 140). The following morning, you might slide an egg on it (see page 210).

SET A BOX GRATER OVER A MEDIUM BOWL AND grate the tomato from the cut sides until all you have left is skin. You should have 1 cup tomato puree.

Combine the oil, green peppers, and red peppers in a large stockpot. Set over medium heat and cook, stirring frequently, until softened, about 15 minutes. Add the onions and garlic. Stir well and continue cooking, stirring frequently, until the onions have softened and become translucent, about 7 minutes.

Add the eggplant, tomato paste, thyme, rosemary, and tomato puree. Stir well until everything is evenly mixed. Cook until sizzling, stirring occasionally, then reduce the heat to low, and continue cooking until very soft, about 1 hour. As you get toward the end of cooking, you have to stir more frequently because the vegetables are losing their moisture, so they tend to stick a little more. Lower the heat if needed.

Season with 1¼ teaspoons salt and ¼ teaspoon pepper. Discard the rosemary and thyme. Taste and add more salt and pepper if you'd like.

The Pisto Manchego can be refrigerated in an airtight container for up to 1 week. Reheat before serving.

*Berenjenas Fritas*

# FRIED EGGPLANT WITH HONEY AND ROSEMARY

**SERVES 4 AS A SMALL PLATE**

Traditionally, this Andalusian dish is served with cane syrup, but I think honey has a more complex flavor. Throughout Spain, there's a range of honey as varied as the landscape. Any type accents the salty crisp shell of these eggplant rounds. My personal touch here is the rosemary, which bridges the savory bite of eggplant with the sweetness of honey. The salty-sweet crunch of this dish makes it the ideal appetizer to any summer or early fall meal.

2 to 3 cups whole milk

1 medium eggplant

2 to 3 cups vegetable oil

½ cup all-purpose flour

Kosher salt

¼ cup honey

1 rosemary sprig

POUR THE MILK INTO A MEDIUM BOWL. TRIM THE top and bottom of the eggplant, then peel. Cut the eggplant into ⅜-inch-thick slices. As you slice the eggplant, put the slices into the bowl with the milk. You should get about 12 slices, but it's fine to have more or less. The milk should cover the eggplant. If it doesn't, add more. Weigh down the eggplant with a heavy plate that fits snugly over the bowl to keep the eggplant submerged. Cover with plastic wrap and soak overnight in the refrigerator.

When ready to cook, fill a large skillet with the vegetable oil. It should be about ½ inch deep; if not, add more. Heat the oil over medium heat until an instant-read thermometer registers 350°F. A pinch of flour should sizzle when it hits the oil.

Spread the flour on a plate. Drain the eggplant. Dredge a slice in the flour and tap off the excess. Carefully drop into the hot oil. Repeat with more eggplant slices, being careful to not crowd the pan. Fry, turning once, until golden brown, 2 to 3 minutes per side. The eggplant shouldn't get too dark; reduce the heat if needed. Transfer to a wire rack to drain and immediately sprinkle with salt and drizzle with honey. Repeat with the remaining eggplant and flour.

Arrange the eggplant on a serving plate. Top each piece with 2 to 3 rosemary leaves. Serve immediately.

# WILTED SPINACH WITH PINE NUTS, RAISINS, AND APPLE

**SERVES 4 TO 6 AS A SMALL PLATE**

In Catalonia, simply cooked leafy greens are made more exciting with the addition of raisins and pine nuts. Raisins are dried from the region's grapevines, pine nuts harvested from the forests, and greens grown in the fertile fields. That trio is now a staple of Catalan cuisine. I decided to add a creamy toasted pine-nut puree for richness and sautéed apples for a juicy crunch. Getting a bit of everything in each bite will change the way you look at spinach. Just don't overcook the greens to make the most of their accompaniments.

¾ cup pine nuts

6 tablespoons blended oil, divided

Kosher salt

¼ cup raisins, preferably Flame raisins

1 lemon, halved

1 small or ½ large sweet-tart apple, preferably Honeycrisp

¼ cup minced shallot

½ cup dry sherry wine

1 pound baby spinach

**P**REHEAT THE OVEN TO 350°F.

Spread the pine nuts on a half-sheet pan and toast until golden brown, 8 to 10 minutes. Cool completely on the pan.

Transfer ½ cup pine nuts to a food processor or blender and add 2 tablespoons oil and a pinch of salt. Puree until smooth, scraping the bowl occasionally. Drizzle half on a serving platter; reserve the remaining for serving.

Squeeze the juice of ½ lemon into a medium bowl. Squeeze 2 teaspoons juice from the other half into a small bowl and reserve the juice and lemon rinds.

Peel, core, and dice the apple and add to the medium bowl with the lemon juice, then add enough cold water to cover. Put the raisins in a small microwave-safe bowl and add enough water to cover by 1 inch. Microwave for 1 minute, then let stand in the hot water until very plumped and tender. Drain the apple and raisins well.

Heat 4 tablespoons oil in a large, deep skillet over medium-high heat. Add the drained raisins and apple and remaining ¼ cup pine nuts. Cook, stirring occasionally, until the apple just begins to soften, 1 to 2 minutes. Add the shallot and cook, stirring, until soft, about 1 minute.

Add the sherry, reserved 2 teaspoons lemon juice, and 1 teaspoon salt and bring to simmer. Add as much spinach as will fit in your pan and toss with tongs as it wilts. As the spinach wilts, keep adding more until all of it has been added. This will take a couple of minutes altogether. You just want the spinach to wilt, not to cook any further. Quickly toss the spinach with all of the sauce and fruit and pine nuts.

Immediately spoon the spinach mixture on top of the pine-nut puree and top with the remaining reserved pine nut puree. Zest half of the reserved lemon rind on top and serve immediately.

*Migas de Verduras*

# SAUTÉED BREAD CRUMBS WITH CAULIFLOWER AND BRUSSELS SPROUTS

❦

**SERVES 4 TO 6 AS A SMALL PLATE**

Migas, which means "bread crumbs," originated as a dish cooked by shepherds out in the fields. They crumbled stale bread and cooked it in animal fat. That two-ingredient recipe evolved into bread cooked with chorizo, ham, or pork and seasoned with herbs and spices. I'm now keeping the bread, but taking the meat out altogether. Inspiration hit me when my chef de cuisine, Frank Muller, tested out a cauliflower dish. When I saw how his fried florets looked like classic migas, I began experimenting. Roasting the cauliflower, along with Brussels sprouts, helped caramelize the vegetables, while finely diced baguette delivered even more crunch than crumbs. At the restaurant, we serve this over Celery Root Puree (page 164), as a small plate, but a larger portion could also work as a vegetarian main course.

½ cup raisins

½ large (3-pound) cauliflower

¼ cup plus 5 teaspoons blended oil, divided

Kosher salt

1 pound Brussels sprouts, trimmed and cut in halves

One 5-inch piece baguette, crusts removed, cut into ¼-inch dice (1 cup)

2 large garlic cloves, minced

1 lemon

POSITION RACKS IN THE UPPER AND LOWER thirds of the oven and preheat to 400°F.

Put the raisins in a small microwave-safe bowl and add enough water to cover by 1 inch. Microwave for 1 minute, then let stand in the hot water until very plumped and tender. Drain well.

Cut the cauliflower florets off the stalks; discard the stalks. Cut the florets into ¼- to ½-inch pieces. You want to use all of the florets, even the crumbs. You should end up with 2 cups.

Line 2 half-sheet pans with foil. Toss the cauliflower with 3 teaspoons oil and ¼ teaspoon salt on one pan. Spread in a single layer. Repeat with the Brussels sprouts on the other pan with 2 teaspoons oil and ¼ teaspoon salt. Turn all the sprouts cut-sides down. Place the Brussels sprouts on the lower oven rack and the cauliflower on the upper rack. Roast until tender and dark golden brown, about 30 minutes.

Place a paper towel-lined plate and slotted spoon next to the stovetop. Heat the remaining ¼ cup oil in a large cast-iron or other heavy skillet over high heat until hot. When you drop a bread cube in, it should sizzle immediately. Add the bread cubes and spread in an even layer. Toss in the oil to evenly coat, then sprinkle with ¼ teaspoon salt. Cook, tossing frequently, until golden brown on most sides and crispy, about 3 minutes. Transfer to the paper towel-lined plate with the slotted spoon to drain.

Return the skillet to medium-high heat. There should still be a thin film of oil in the bottom of the pan. Add the garlic and cook, stirring, until fragrant and just starting to turn golden brown, about 1 minute. Don't let the garlic burn.

Lift the foil with the sprouts and cauliflower to dump them into the skillet. Add the raisins and bread cubes. Cook, stirring, until well-mixed, about 1 minute. Remove from the heat and zest half of the lemon on top. Toss once more and season with ¼ teaspoon salt. Taste and add more salt if you'd like.

*Puré de Ráiz Apio*

# CELERY ROOT PUREE

MAKES 3 CUPS;

SERVES 8 TO 12 AS A SMALL PLATE

Two flavors I love are the anise notes of celery root and the tartness of plain Greek yogurt. I found that those flavors work well together when blended into an airy puree. Because celery root is still quite starchy, a final squirt of lemon juice lightens the mix.

1 large celery root (1½ pounds), generously trimmed and peeled and cut into ½-inch dice

1 large garlic clove, peeled and smashed

6 sprigs thyme

1 cup half-and-half

1 cup whole milk

4 tablespoons unsalted butter, room temperature

⅔ cup 2% plain Greek yogurt, room temperature

¼ teaspoon fresh lemon juice

1½ teaspoons kosher salt

COMBINE THE CELERY ROOT, GARLIC, THYME, half-and-half, and milk in a 4-quart saucepan. Bring to a boil over medium-high heat. Reduce the heat to low and simmer until the celery root is super soft, about 25 minutes. When you pierce one with a fork, it should fall apart and split in half. Get it on a really low simmer because the cream evaporates quickly. Remove and discard the thyme sprigs.

Immediately transfer the mixture to a blender. Whenever you mash or puree anything, you have to do it while it's hot. Puree until very smooth, then add the butter and process again until very smooth. Add the yogurt, lemon juice, and salt. Puree until very smooth. If you don't have a powerful high-speed blender and the mixture can't get going, you need to take out half of the mixture and puree, then transfer to your serving bowl and then puree the remaining until very smooth. You'll need to scrape down the sides of the blender occasionally. Serve hot.

*Puré de Patatas y Aceite de Oliva*

# OLIVE OIL POTATO PUREE

MAKES 4 CUPS;

SERVES 4 TO 8 AS A SMALL PLATE

Swapping in olive oil for butter in classic mashed potatoes adds complex fruity notes, particularly if you use oil pressed from Arbequina olives. My favorites are California Olive Ranch's Arbequina or Miller's blends, but you should use whatever you like. Lighter than buttery mashed potatoes but just as rich in taste, these potatoes are the perfect base for just about anything from octopus (see page 77) to oxtail (see page 112).

2 pounds Yukon gold potatoes (about 6 large), peeled and cut into 1-inch chunks

½ cup heavy cream

½ cup extra-virgin olive oil

Kosher salt

PLACE THE POTATOES IN A 4-QUART SAUCEPAN and cover with cold water by 1 inch. Bring to a boil over high heat. Reduce the heat to keep a steady boil. Cook until the potatoes are very tender, about 15 minutes. When you pierce a potato with a fork, it should break in half.

Drain well, then return to the pan. Cook over medium-high heat, stirring to release some of the moisture, until they look dry, about 1 minute. You're not trying to color them at all.

Microwave the cream in a liquid measuring cup until really hot but not boiling, about 1½ minutes.

Pass the potatoes through a food mill or ricer into a large bowl. You could also mash them by hand with a fork or potato masher. The texture won't be quite as smooth but pretty close.

Fold the hot cream into the potatoes. Fold in the oil a couple tablespoons at a time. You can't add it all at once because you need the fat to blend into the potatoes and not separate. Season with 1 teaspoon salt, then taste and add more salt if you'd like. Serve hot.

The potatoes can be refrigerated in an airtight container for up to 1 week. As they chill, they stiffen. When ready to eat, stir them in a saucepan over low heat with a little more cream, olive oil, and salt to return them to their original consistency.

*Papas Arrugadas con Mojo Verde*

# SALTED POTATOES WITH HERB SAUCE

SERVES 4 TO 6 AS A SMALL PLATE

Originally from the Canary Islands, this recipe calls for cooking potatoes in the seawater that surrounds the islands. As the water evaporates, the residual salt dries into a crust around the spuds. Here, you're mimicking the ocean with a very well-salted pot of water. The herb sauce usually only has cilantro, garlic, and oil, but I like the depth of flavor you get by mixing in parsley and a little oregano and cumin.

### MOJO VERDE

**1 cup packed fresh cilantro leaves**

**½ cup packed fresh flat-leaf parsley leaves**

**3 garlic cloves, peeled**

**2 tablespoons fresh oregano leaves**

**½ cup extra-virgin olive oil**

**1 tablespoon sherry vinegar**

**¾ teaspoon kosher salt**

**½ teaspoon ground cumin**

### POTATOES

**2 pounds mixed baby potatoes (1-inch round), scrubbed**

**¼ cup kosher salt**

TO MAKE THE MOJO VERDE, PROCESS ALL OF THE ingredients in a food processor until smooth, scraping the bowl occasionally. The herbs will be finely chopped and the sauce may look a bit broken.

To make the potatoes, cover them with 6 cups water in a large saucepan and add the salt. Bring to a boil over high heat, stirring to dissolve the salt. Reduce the heat to steadily boil until extremely tender, about 30 minutes. Drain all but ¼ cup of the cooking liquid. Cook over medium-high heat, shaking the pan every few seconds, until the liquid evaporates. In the process, the potatoes will become coated in a crystal white shell of salt. Keep cooking until the saucepan is bone dry and the potatoes are covered evenly with salt. Transfer to a large bowl and shake and toss the potatoes to remove any excess salt. The crystals will flake off.

Serve immediately with the mojo verde.

*Patatas Bravas*

# ROASTED POTATOES WITH BRAVA SAUCE AND ALLIOLI

SERVES 6 TO 8 AS A SMALL PLATE

You'll find this Spanish counterpart to American French fries all over Spain. There—and at the restaurant—the potatoes are deep-fried. But I like to roast the potatoes at home. (If you'd like to deep fry at home, you can cook the potatoes in 300°F oil until just tender, drain and chill them, then fry them again at 375°F until crunchy.)

What I haven't altered are the essential condiments: brava sauce and allioli. The smoky sweet tomato sauce and garlicky mayonnaise make the crunchy potatoes one of my favorite Spanish dishes. They're the appetizer, side, or snack you can eat with anything.

### BRAVA SAUCE

1 tablespoon blended oil

1½ teaspoons minced garlic

1 arbol chile, crushed into bits, or ¼ teaspoon crushed red pepper

1 tablespoon tomato paste

1 tablespoon sherry vinegar

¾ cup canned crushed San Marzano tomatoes

1 tablespoon granulated sugar

1¼ teaspoons pimentón (sweet smoked paprika)

¼ teaspoon kosher salt

### POTATOES

2 pounds Idaho potatoes, peeled and cut into ¾-inch chunks

¼ cup blended oil

Kosher salt

Allioli (page 182) for serving

TO MAKE THE BRAVA SAUCE, COMBINE THE OIL, garlic, and chile in a small saucepan. Cook over medium heat, stirring, until fragrant, about 15 seconds. Add the tomato paste and sherry vinegar. Cook, stirring, until the vinegar has evaporated, about 1 minute. Add the tomatoes and sugar and reduce the heat to low. Cook, stirring occasionally, until thickened and the flavors have melded together, about 30 minutes. Stir in the pimentón and salt.

Transfer to a blender or food processor and puree until very smooth, scraping the bowl occasionally. Add water, 1 teaspoon at a time, until the mixture achieves a ketchup-like consistency that you can almost drizzle, but is still quite thick. Keep at room temperature if serving immediately. The sauce can be refrigerated in an airtight container for up to 2 weeks.

To make the potatoes, preheat the oven to 475°F with a half-sheet pan on the center rack.

Toss the potatoes with the oil and 1 teaspoon salt in a large bowl. When the oven has fully heated, carefully spread the potatoes on the hot pan in a single layer, scraping all the oil in the bowl onto the pan.

Roast until the bottoms are deeply browned and release easily from the pan, about 20 minutes. Carefully flip the potatoes and roast until the other sides brown, 10 to 20 minutes. Sprinkle with ½ teaspoon salt and transfer to a serving platter.

Serve the potatoes, with the brava sauce and allioli, either in bowls for dipping or distributed on top using squirt bottles or resealable plastic bags with small holes snipped in the corners.

*Papas Aliñas*

# POTATO SALAD with FRESH HERBS

SERVES 6 TO 8 AS A SMALL PLATE

This potato salad from Andalucía gets dressed in sherry vinegar and oil while hot to fully absorb the seasonings. It's a simple way to make potatoes tasty. The dressed potatoes can be refrigerated for up to three days and tossed with the aromatics and herbs just before serving. Fresh herbs are not traditional in this dish, but I really love the blend of chives, tarragon, dill, and parsley. This salad would be ideal at any cookout, but is especially good with boquerónes, marinated white anchovies you can buy at well-stocked markets.

24 ounces (2-inch-round) red new potatoes, scrubbed

Kosher salt and freshly ground black pepper

2 tablespoons extra-virgin olive oil

1 tablespoon reserve sherry vinegar

¼ cup thinly sliced red onion

1 tablespoon minced chives

1 tablespoon coarsely chopped fresh tarragon leaves

1 tablespoon coarsely chopped fresh dill

1 tablespoon coarsely chopped fresh flat-leaf parsley leaves

COVER THE POTATOES WITH COLD WATER BY 2 inches in a large saucepan and add 2 tablespoons salt. Bring to a boil over high heat, then reduce the heat to boil steadily until tender but not falling apart, 20 to 30 minutes. Drain well. When cool enough to handle, cut in quarters.

Toss the potatoes with the oil, vinegar, and 1 teaspoon salt. Season with pepper. Refrigerate until room temperature, cool, or cold.

When ready to serve, toss with the onion, chives, tarragon, dill, and parsley. Taste and add salt and pepper if you'd like. Serve immediately.

*Pimientos del Piquillo Confitados*

# CONFIT PIQUILLO PEPPERS

❧

**SERVES 6 TO 8 AS AN ACCOMPANIMENT**

Jarred piquillo peppers already come tender and juicy. After a low and slow bake in oil, they become meltingly soft and infused with garlic, rosemary, and thyme. They're wonderful simply spooned onto bread but also good with any grilled meat or in sandwiches. If you're storing them, keep them covered with the oil. Otherwise, save the oil to dress salads or drizzle over vegetables.

2 (12-ounce) jars piquillo peppers, drained

8 garlic cloves, lightly smashed and peeled

2 large sprigs rosemary

8 sprigs thyme

Kosher salt

Blended oil, as needed

**P**REHEAT THE OVEN TO 300°F.
Arrange the peppers in an even layer in a 9- by 13- by 2-inch baking dish. Evenly scatter the garlic, rosemary, and thyme on top, then sprinkle with 1 teaspoon salt. Add enough oil to cover the peppers.

Cover the dish with foil and bake until the peppers are extremely tender and almost falling apart, about 2½ hours.

Uncover and cool in the dish on a rack. When cool enough to handle, discard the herbs and very carefully transfer the peppers and garlic to serving plates. Save any leftover peppers and the fragrant oil in airtight containers in the refrigerator for up to 2 weeks.

173

# STUFFED PIQUILLO PEPPERS

## MAKES 12

Piquillos, sweet red peppers, seem almost designed to be stuffed because of their conical shape. They're sold wood-fire roasted and peeled so they have a smoky, juicy sweetness and are tender. When stuffed, they can be served individually as appetizers, in pairs as a small plate, or in trios or more for a light meal along with good bread and a salad.

| | |
|---|---|
| 12 whole piquillos, seeds carefully removed, peppers patted very dry | Fillings (recipes follow)<br><br>1 tablespoon extra-virgin olive oil |

FILL THE PIQUILLOS AS INSTRUCTED. THE FILLED piquillos can be refrigerated in an airtight container for up to 2 days before cooking.

When ready to serve, heat the oil in a large skillet over medium-high heat until hot but not smoking. Add the stuffed piquillos in a single layer and cook, turning once, until browned on the outside and hot inside, 1 to 2 minutes per side. A small offset spatula works well for turning the piquillos. Serve hot.

## JAMÓN SERRANO AND MAHÓN

PULL OR CUT 6 VERY THIN SLICES SERRANO HAM IN half lengthwise. Use a vegetable peeler or cheese plane to shave 6 ounces Mahón cheese. Divide the cheese among the ham slices, laying the shavings over the ham, overlapping if needed. Roll up each piece of ham, spiraling in the cheese, then stuff each ham roll into a piquillo.

## CAPRICHO DE CABRA

CUT 6 OUNCES CAPRICHO DE CABRA OR OTHER fresh goat cheese into 12 pieces. Roll each piece into a conical shape about ¼ inch shorter than the length of the piquillos. Slide each piece into a piquillo.

## BRANDADA

PLACE ¾ CUP BRANDADA (PAGE 34) INTO A HEAVY-duty resealable plastic bag. Snip a ½-inch hole in one corner, then squeeze 1 tablespoon brandada into each piquillo.

*Setas al Jerez*

# MUSHROOMS SAUTÉED IN SHERRY

**SERVES 4 TO 6 AS A SMALL PLATE**

In Jerez, sherry ends up in countless dishes and is often cooked with mushrooms, which readily soak up the woodsy alcohol. To intensify that classic dish, I've created a shortcut mushroom stock here that simply simmers dried mushrooms in water. I'm so happy with how much earthy mushroom flavor the stock develops in only five minutes. The stock turns this into a quick side dish that can come together even faster if you find cleaned and cut mushrooms in your store. The seared and saucy mushrooms make a great accompaniment to any kind of meat, especially grilled steak (see page 103).

1 ounce dried porcini mushrooms

1 pound fresh mixed mushrooms, such as oysters, shiitakes, and creminis, divided

8 tablespoons blended oil, divided

3 tablespoons minced shallot

6 thyme sprigs

½ cup dry sherry wine

1 teaspoon kosher salt

BRING THE DRIED PORCINIS AND 1 CUP WATER TO a boil in a small saucepan. Reduce the heat to low and simmer for 5 minutes. Remove from the heat and strain through a fine-mesh sieve, pressing on the solids to extract as much liquid as possible. Discard the solids. You will be left with an intense rich dried mushroom stock.

Clean the mixed mushrooms by gently brushing the dirt away with paper towels. Do not wash them with water because this makes them much more difficult to sear. If they are extremely sandy or dirty and you have to use water, put them in a salad spinner to dry them out as much as possible before proceeding. Trim the cleaned mushrooms and cut into 1-inch pieces.

Heat 2 tablespoons oil in a large skillet over high heat until very hot and almost smoking. Add one-quarter of the mushrooms in a single layer and cook, turning every once in a while, until seared to nice deep golden brown, 3 to 4 minutes. Transfer to a bowl. Repeat with the remaining mushroom in three batches, replenishing the skillet with 2 tablespoons oil for each batch.

Reduce the heat to medium-high and return all the mushrooms to the skillet. Add the shallot and thyme and cook until the shallot has softened, 1 to 2 minutes. Then add the mushroom stock and salt, bring to a simmer, and cook until almost all the liquid has evaporated, stirring often, about 2 minutes. It is important that you take the stock until it's almost dry, but not so far that the skillet starts to burn. Add the sherry and reduce again until almost dry, about 3 minutes.

Transfer to a dish and serve hot.

# NOODLES, RICE, AND BEANS

*Rossejat Negro*

# SQUID INK PASTA

**SERVES 8**

Rossejar means "to toast" and that's the first step in these paella-like noodle dishes. Noodles are not commonly found in Spanish cuisine, but they form the basis of this Catalan specialty. Very fine noodles—Spanish fideos or broken vermicelli or angel hair all work—are browned in oil before simmering later. Not only do the noodles develop a richer taste, but they also hold an al dente texture even after a long simmer.

While noodles are unique to Catalonia, the combination of squid with its ink is found all over the country. Squid ink is available at specialty stores and is a must here. Its flavor is subtle but tastes purely of the ocean. Once you buy that ingredient, the whole meal comes together quickly. It's ideal with a glass of white Garnacha from Catalonia's Mediterranean coast.

4 tablespoons plus 2 teaspoons extra-virgin olive oil, divided

1 pound angel hair pasta, broken into 1-inch-long pieces

1 pound squid tubes and tentacles, tentacles cut in half, tubes cut into ¼-inch rings, patted very dry

Kosher salt

1 garlic clove, minced

½ small onion, finely chopped (¼ cup)

1 (14.5-ounce) can crushed San Marzano tomatoes

4 cups Seafood Stock (page 183) or store-bought unsalted seafood stock, heated

2 teaspoons squid ink

½ teaspoon pimentón (sweet smoked paprika)

Allioli (page 182) for serving

HEAT 2 TABLESPOONS OIL IN A 16-INCH PAELLA pan or cast-iron pan over high heat until hot but not smoking. Add the noodles and immediately stir to evenly coat the noodles with the oil before they start browning. Continue cooking, stirring and tossing frequently, until golden brown, about 5 minutes. Transfer to a large bowl. Alternatively, toss the noodles with 2 tablespoons oil and spread in a half-sheet pan. Bake in a 350°F oven, stirring occasionally, until golden brown. It's a matter of whether you'd rather scrape the noodles out of the paella pan or turn on the oven. Both techniques work well.

Add 2 tablespoons oil to the paella pan and reduce the heat to medium-high. Add the squid and sprinkle with ½ teaspoon salt. Cook, turning and tossing, until starting to turn golden brown, about 2 minutes. Add the remaining 2 teaspoons oil and reduce the heat to medium. Add the minced garlic. Cook, stirring, until fragrant, about 15 seconds. Stir in the onion and cook, stirring, until translucent and soft, about 2 minutes. Add the tomatoes and cook, stirring often, until the tomatoes turn a dark brick red and start to stick to the bottom of the pan, about 5 minutes.

Stir in the noodles, then the hot stock, squid ink, pimentón, and 2½ teaspoons salt. Stir well and bring to a boil over medium-high heat, stirring continuously. Spread the noodles in an even layer. Now don't touch it. You want to cook the noodles until they're just tender and stick to the bottom of the pan and make a snap, crackle, pop noise, about 7 minutes. Remove from the heat and serve with the allioli.

*(Continued)*

*Allioli*

———

# GARLIC MAYONNAISE

### MAKES ABOUT 1 CUP

Allioli derives from "all i oli." In Catalan, "all" means garlic, "i" means and, and "oli" means oil. Those are the only ingredients in the most traditional version of this sauce. You mortar-and-pestle the garlic and then add the oil drop by drop while whisking with the pestle until you get the consistency of mayonnaise. It's difficult and time-consuming. But when you're in someone's home in Spain or at a great restaurant, you can taste the difference. You can even see it. Even though it's as thick as mayonnaise, it's not quite as smooth. I've never tried that technique because I just don't have the patience.

My whole take on allioli speaks to my practical side and tastes delicious. For a fool-proof and fast allioli, I use a food processor. The feed tube with the insert slows the flow of the oil to just the right drip for the emul-sification. I use a whole egg, because I hate having leftover whites, and a blended oil, to avoid getting out both my canola oil and olive oil. (If you can't find blended oil, do half-and-half canola and a mild-flavored olive oil, such as Arbequina.)

A good allioli will leave you breathing garlic four hours later. Even so, garlic varies widely in intensity. Take a tiny nibble of your clove, then use anywhere from one small clove to two large ones, depending on the potency.

This all-purpose recipe beats mayonnaise in any sandwich, serves as a sauce for rosse-jat, paella, potatoes, and beans, and as a dip for vegetables or a spread for meat.

1 large egg

1 to 2 garlic cloves, peeled and smashed

1¼ teaspoons fresh lemon juice

¼ teaspoon kosher salt

1 cup blended oil

COMBINE THE EGG, GARLIC, LEMON JUICE, AND salt in a food processor. Turn the machine on and pour a little of the oil through the slow-drip feed tube. Add the remaining oil and process until it's all emulsified into the mixture.

To make by hand, push the garlic through a garlic press, then whisk with the lemon juice, salt, and egg. Whisk in the oil, a drop at a time, to ensure an emulsification that doesn't break.

Or the allioli can be refrigerated in an airtight container for up to 1 week.

*Rossejat*

# SHRIMP PASTA

SERVES 8

This variation on the Rossejat Negro (page 180) is just as simple, but highlights shrimp instead of squid. When I have time, I make a stock with the shrimp shells as well as the fish bones. When I'm busy, I use store-bought seafood or fish stock. A high-quality one will taste as full-bodied as homemade, and you'll still get plenty of savory seafood flavor from the shrimp.

### SEAFOOD STOCK

1 pound
(30/34-count)
shell-on shrimp
(about 32)

1 tablespoon
blended oil

1 small fresh tomato,
cored and coarsely
chopped

½ large carrot,
coarsely chopped

½ green bell
pepper, coarsely
chopped

2 garlic cloves,
smashed and peeled

1 pound fish bones,
cut into 2-inch
pieces

1 sprig flat-leaf
parsley

1 fresh or dried bay
leaf

5 black peppercorns

### ROSSEJAT

3 tablespoons plus 2
teaspoons blended
oil, divided

1 pound angel hair
pasta, broken into
1-inch-long pieces

2 tablespoons
packed minced garlic

¼ cup minced yellow
onion (from about ½
small)

1 (14.5-ounce) can
crushed San
Marzano tomatoes

½ teaspoon
pimentón (sweet
smoked paprika)

Allioli (recipe
opposite) for serving

TO MAKE THE SEAFOOD STOCK, PEEL AND DEVEIN the shrimp. Refrigerate the shrimp for the rossejat. Reserve the shells for the stock. If you're making the Rossejat Negro (page 180) you can omit the shrimp shells.

Combine the oil, tomato, carrot, pepper, and garlic in a large saucepan. Stir well and set over medium-high heat. When the vegetables start to sizzle, reduce the heat to medium and cook, stirring occasionally, until the fresh tomato has broken down and is starting to caramelize on the bottom of the pan, about 13 minutes. Add the shrimp shells, raise the heat to medium, and cook, stirring, until the shells are bright pink, about 2 minutes. Add the fish bones, parsley, bay leaf, peppercorns, and 5 cups water. The liquid should just cover the fish bones. Bring to a boil over high heat. Reduce the heat to maintain a bare simmer and simmer for 1 hour.

Strain the stock through a fine-mesh sieve into a saucepot, pressing on the solids to extract as much liquid as possible. You should have 4 cups stock. You want it to be really hot when you add it to the noodles, so keep it over low heat.

To make the rossejat, heat 2 tablespoons oil in a 16-inch paella pan or cast-iron pan over high heat until hot but not smoking. Add the noodles and immediately stir to evenly coat the noodles with the oil before they start browning. Continue cooking, stirring and tossing frequently, until golden brown, about 5 minutes. Transfer to a large bowl. Alternatively, toss the noodles with 2 tablespoons oil and spread in a half-sheet pan. Bake in a 350°F oven, stirring occasionally, until golden brown. It's a matter of whether you'd rather scrape the noodles out of the paella pan or turn on the oven. Both techniques work well.

Wipe out the skillet, add 1 teaspoon oil, and turn the heat to medium-high. Add half the reserved shrimp and sprinkle with ½ teaspoon salt. Cook, turning and tossing, until just curled and orange, about 1 minute. Transfer to a plate. Repeat with another teaspoon oil and the remaining shrimp.

Wipe out the skillet, add the remaining table-spoon oil, and turn the heat to medium. Add the garlic. Cook, stirring occasionally, until fragrant and starting to turn golden but not burn, about 2 minutes. Stir in the onion and cook, stirring, until translucent and soft, about 1 minute. Add

*(Continued)*

the canned tomatoes and cook, stirring frequently, until the tomatoes turn a dark brick red and start to stick to the bottom of the pan, about 5 minutes.

Stir in the noodles, then the hot stock, pimentón, and 2½ teaspoons salt. Stir well and bring to a boil over medium-high heat, stirring continuously. Spread the noodles in an even layer and nestle the shrimp on top of the mixture. Now don't touch it. You want to cook the noodles until they're just tender and stick to the bottom of the pan and make a snap, crackle, pop noise, about 7 minutes. Remove from the heat and serve with the allioli.

# PAELLA

DURING A COSTA BRAVA BEACH VACATION, I HAD the best paella ever. When I asked the cook how he did it, he went on and on about the stock. He didn't talk about the rice or the just-caught seafood; he focused on the one ingredient you can't even see in the finished dish. As he expounded upon the ingredients that went into it and the time it took, it struck me: Spaniards take pride in how long their cooking takes, both in terms of actual simmering hours, but also in terms of the years it takes to master a dish. This cook has spent over 25 years perfecting paella. His primary job is actually as a fisherman, so he gets to turn out paella with the best and freshest possible ingredients, namely his daily catch.

Even though that paella was made in Catalonia, the dish itself originated in Valencia. The word paella refers to the pan, derived from the Latin word for pan, "patella," but now is synonymous with the rice dish found all over Spain. Valencia was the dish's birthplace because it is home to wetlands ideal for growing the short grain rice needed for the dish. In fact, the only specialty items you need to make paella are Spanish short-grain rice, such as bomba, and a paella pan, which creates a charred crust, called the soccarat, on the bottom. (I especially like the heavy duty Pata Negra pans.)

Once you have the right rice and pan, you can cook the rice in stock or tomato sauce or both, and you can add any combination of meat, seafood, or vegetables. The Valencian classic combines locally sourced rabbit, snails, and vegetables. In my versions, I follow that spirit of local cooking when choosing ingredients. Because paella already has a rice base, it's the ideal one-dish meal, even for entertaining. I don't bother to serve anything else aside from plenty of sangria, wine, or beer.

Both grill and stovetop-oven techniques work, but the smokiness from outdoor cooking is incomparable. It actually isn't more complicated than the indoor version. Paella technique lends itself to live fire cooking: It needs to start over high heat, then scale down to medium and, eventually, medium-low. As the coals burn, they'll naturally diminish in heat, right at the times you need. I've made paella in grills countless times and remain amazed at how consistently this holds true.

The real appeal to cooking paella outdoors is being able to hang out with friends while creating a huge family meal that you'll dig into together. It isn't just a meal you make and serve, it's one you share from start to finish.

Vegetable Paelila (p. 191)

*Paella de Verduras*

# VEGETABLE PAELLA

I wanted to create a paella that celebrates fall. During a trip to the farmers' market, I gathered everything that looked good and turned it into a deeply satisfying vegetarian main course. The roasted garlic and caramelized vegetables mimic the depth of meat, as do mushrooms. You can skip the roasted garlic for sliced fresh cloves if you're in a rush and still end up with delicious results.

| 20- TO 22-INCH PAELLA PAN (SERVES 10 TO 12) | 16- TO 18-INCH PAELLA PAN (SERVES 6 TO 8) |
| --- | --- |
| 2 heads garlic | 1 head garlic |
| 1 ounce dried porcini mushrooms (1 cup) | ½ ounce dried porcini mushrooms (½ cup) |
| 6 cups water | 3 cups water |
| 15 tablespoons extra-virgin olive oil, divided | 7.5 tablespoons extra-virgin olive oil, divided |
| 2 pounds mixed mushrooms, such as cremini, shiitakes, and oysters, cut into 1-inch pieces | 1 pound mixed mushrooms, such as cremini, shiitakes, and oysters, cut into 1-inch pieces |
| 3 tablespoons kosher salt, divided | 1½ tablespoons kosher salt, divided |
| 1 pound Brussels sprouts, trimmed and halved | 8 ounces Brussels sprouts, trimmed and halved |
| 1 large acorn squash, peeled and cut into large chunks (4 cups) | 1 small acorn squash, peeled and cut into large chunks (2 cups) |
| 1 medium eggplant, peeled and cut into large chunks (4 cups) | 1 very small eggplant, peeled and cut into large chunks (2 cups) |
| 1 large onion, finely chopped | 1 small onion, finely chopped |
| 2 cups canned crushed San Marzano tomatoes | 1 cup canned crushed San Marzano tomatoes |
| 2 cups dry sherry wine | 1 cup dry sherry wine |
| 2 tablespoons pimentón (smoked sweet paprika) | 1 tablespoon pimentón (smoked sweet paprika) |
| ½ teaspoon saffron threads | ¼ teaspoon saffron threads |
| 1 fresh or dried bay leaf | 1 fresh or dried bay leaf |
| 2 cups bomba, calasparra, or Arborio rice | 1 cup bomba, calasparra, or Arborio rice |
| 6 sage sprigs | 3 sage sprigs |
| 12 thyme sprigs | 6 thyme sprigs |

**P**REHEAT THE OVEN TO 325°F. CUT THE VERY TOPS off the heads of garlic, then place back over the garlic. Wrap tightly in foil, then bake on a rimmed baking sheet until very tender, about 1 hour. When cool enough to handle, discard the tops and squeeze the cloves out into a small bowl. If using the oven variation below, raise the oven temperature to 350°F. Otherwise, turn off the oven.

Bring the dried mushrooms and water to a boil in a medium saucepan. Cover, remove from the heat, and let stand for 30 minutes. Drain through a fine-mesh sieve, pressing on the mushrooms to extract as much liquid as possible. Reserve the mushroom stock and discard the mushrooms.

Prepare an outdoor grill that will fit your paella pan. If you have a standard round kettle grill, the handles of the paella pan may prevent the pan from sitting directly on the rack. It's okay as long as the base of the pan is smaller than the grill grate. Heat enough wood or coals to completely cover the bottom of the grill until very hot.

Carefully place the pan on the grill and add 3 (or 1½) tablespoons oil. Heat until the oil and pan are very hot. Add the mixed mushrooms in a single layer and cook, turning once or twice, until nicely browned around the edges, about 5 minutes. Season with 1 (or ½) teaspoon salt, then transfer to a very large bowl. Repeat the same process with the Brussels sprouts, squash, and eggplant, using 3 (or 1½ tablespoons) oil each time and seasonings with 1 (or ½) teaspoon salt at the end of cooking. All of the vegetables can go into the same bowl.

Heat another 3 (or 1½) tablespoons oil and add the onion. Cook, stirring often, until soft, about 3 minutes. Season with 1 (or ½) teaspoon salt, then add the roasted garlic and tomatoes. Cook, stirring occasionally, until the liquid has evaporated and the tomatoes are starting to caramelize, about 10 minutes. Return all the vegetables to the pan.

Add the sherry and cook, stirring, until almost all of the liquid has evaporated, then stir in the pimentón, saffron, bay leaf, and mushroom stock. Bring to a simmer and stir in the remaining salt. Stir in the rice until evenly distributed around the pan. Make sure all the grains are submerged in the liquid. Scatter the sage and thyme on top.

Cover, with the grill vents open, and simmer until the rice is tender and the liquid has evaporated, 10 to 20 minutes. The cooking time will depend on how hot your fire is at this point and the type of rice you use. The bottom of the rice should be browned and crusty, too.

Wearing heavy-duty oven mitts, transfer the pan to a heatproof surface or very large cooling rack. Tent with foil and let stand for 10 minutes. Serve hot.

**OVEN PAELLA:** To make this in the oven, position a rack in the bottom of the oven and preheat to 350°F. Follow the instructions above and use a stovetop, straddling the pan between two burners, to sear the vegetables over high heat and sauté the onion and deglaze with the sherry over medium heat. After stirring in the rice and topping with the herbs, transfer to the oven and bake. If the bottom hasn't developed a crust by the time the rice and beans are tender, return to the stovetop and set over high heat. Cook just until a crust forms, then tent with foil and let stand as above before serving.

*Paella de Pollo*

# CHICKEN PAELLA

This is my take on the classic Valencian-style paella that combines rabbit or chicken with snails and beans. I love the creaminess of giant lima beans, especially the ones from Rancho Gordo, a bean company in Northern California. Their earthy sweetness pairs so well with the savory seared chicken and the juicy artichokes. When those three ingredients simmer together, they're essentially creating a stock that will infuse the rice as well.

| 20- TO 22-INCH PAELLA PAN (SERVES 10 TO 12) | 16- TO 18-INCH PAELLA PAN (SERVES 6 TO 8) |
| --- | --- |
| 8 ounces dried large lima beans (1 cup) | 4 ounces dried large lima beans (½ cup) |
| ½ cup extra-virgin olive oil | ¼ cup extra-virgin olive oil |
| 6 chicken legs, thighs and drumsticks split | 3 chicken legs, thighs and drumsticks split |
| 3 tablespoons kosher salt, divided | 1½ tablespoons kosher salt, divided |
| 1 teaspoon freshly ground black pepper | ½ teaspoon freshly ground black pepper |
| 4 artichokes, trimmed to hearts, cut in quarters | 2 artichokes, trimmed to hearts, cut in quarters |
| 12 garlic cloves, peeled and thinly sliced | 6 garlic cloves, peeled and thinly sliced |
| 1 large red bell pepper, thinly sliced | 1 small red bell pepper, thinly sliced |
| 1 large green bell pepper, thinly sliced | 1 small green bell pepper, thinly sliced |
| 1 large onion, finely chopped | 1 small onion, finely chopped |
| 2 cups canned crushed San Marzano tomatoes | 1 cup canned crushed San Marzano tomatoes |
| 2 tablespoons pimentón (smoked sweet paprika) | 1 tablespoon pimentón (smoked sweet paprika) |
| ½ teaspoon saffron threads | ¼ teaspoon saffron threads |
| 6 cups water | 3 cups water |
| 2 cups bomba, calasparra, or Arborio rice | 1 cup bomba, calasparra, or Arborio rice |
| 4 rosemary sprigs | 2 rosemary sprigs |

THE NIGHT BEFORE COOKING, COVER THE LIMA beans with cold water by 3 inches in a large bowl. Cover and refrigerate until ready to cook, then drain well.

Prepare an outdoor grill that will fit your paella pan. If you have a standard round kettle grill, the handles of the paella pan may prevent the pan from sitting directly on the rack. It's okay as long as the base of the pan is smaller than the grill grate. Heat enough wood or coals to completely cover the bottom of the grill until very hot.

Carefully place the pan on the grill and add the oil. Heat until the oil and pan are very hot. Season the chicken with one-third of the salt and all of the pepper. Place in the oil, skin side down. Cook, turning once, until golden brown, about 10 minutes. Transfer to a large plate.

Add the artichokes to the hot oil and cook, turning occasionally, until golden brown, about 5 minutes. Sprinkle with half of the remaining salt and transfer to the plate with the chicken.

Add the garlic to the hot oil and cook, stirring, until golden, about 15 seconds. Add the bell peppers and onion and cook, stirring occasionally, until soft, about 10 minutes. Add the tomatoes and cook, stirring occasionally, until the liquid has evaporated and the tomatoes are starting to caramelize, about 10 minutes. Stir in the pimentón and saffron.

Add the lima beans and water and return the chicken and artichokes to the pan, along with any accumulated juices. Stir in the remaining salt. Bring to a simmer, then simmer for 10 minutes.

Stir in the rice until evenly distributed around the pan. Make sure all the grains are submerged in the liquid. Scatter the rosemary on top. Cover, with the grill vents open, and simmer until the rice and beans are tender and the liquid has evaporated, 10 to 20 minutes. The cooking time will depend on how hot your fire is at this point and the type of rice you use. The bottom of the rice should be browned and crusty, too.

Wearing heavy-duty oven mitts, transfer the pan to a heatproof surface or very large cooling rack. Tent with foil and let stand for 10 minutes. Serve hot.

**OVEN PAELLA:** To make this in the oven, position a rack in the bottom of the oven and preheat to 350°F. Follow the instructions above and use a stovetop, straddling the pan between two burners, to sear the chicken and artichokes over high heat, sauté the vegetables over medium heat, and simmer the beans over low heat. After stirring in the rice and topping with the rosemary, transfer to the oven and bake. If the bottom hasn't developed a crust by the time the rice and beans are tender, return to the stovetop and set over high heat. Cook just until a crust forms, then tent with foil and let stand as above before serving.

# SEAFOOD STEW WITH RICE, FISH, LOBSTER, AND MUSSELS

### SERVES 6 TO 8

Stewier than paella, but not as thin as a soup, suquet hovers between light and hearty. Costa Brava fishermen created this with whatever they caught but knew they couldn't sell, and cooked it into a soup with potatoes. My idea was to turn that soup into a rice dish similar to a classic arroz caldoso (soupy rice) and up it with lobster and mussels.

1 whole (1¼-pound) live lobster

1 whole (1½-pound) snapper or other firm white fish, scaled and gutted

2 tablespoons plus 2 teaspoons canola oil, divided

2 garlic cloves, smashed and peeled

1 onion, chopped

2 ripe tomatoes, chopped

1 teaspoon tomato paste

½ cup dry white wine

1 leek, white part only, thinly sliced

1 celery stalk, chopped

1 carrot, chopped

1 fresh or dried bay leaf

4 saffron threads

1 cup bomba or Arborio rice

Kosher salt

20 mussels, cleaned, beards removed

1 teaspoon white wine vinegar

2 tablespoons minced fresh flat-leaf parsley

CURL THE LOBSTER'S TAIL UNDER AND HOLD IT, along with its body, against a cutting board. Quickly insert a very sharp knife into the center of its head where it meets the body and swiftly bring down the blade between its eyes. Cut through to split the head in half. Twist off the tail and claws, then twist off the knuckles from the claws. Cut the tail in half lengthwise. Remove and discard the vein and digestive tract. Place the tail halves, claws, and knuckles on a dish and reserve in the refrigerator. Save the head to make the stock.

Remove and discard the gills from the fish head. Snip off the fins with kitchen shears and discard. Cut the fillets off the fish, then cut each fillet in thirds. Place on a dish and reserve in the refrigerator. Cut the bones in pieces and reserve, along with the head and tail, for the stock.

Heat 1 tablespoon oil in a large stockpot over medium-high heat. Add the lobster head and fish tail, head, and bones. Cook until well-browned, then turn and cook the other sides, about 5 minutes. Transfer to a bowl. Add 1 tablespoon oil and then the garlic. Cook, stirring, until golden, about 15 seconds. Add the onion and cook, stirring often, until golden brown, about 5 minutes. Add the chopped tomatoes and tomato paste. Cook, stirring often, until most of the liquid has evaporated and the tomatoes begin to caramelize, about 5 minutes. Add the wine and boil until almost all of the liquid has evaporated.

Add the leek, celery, carrot, bay leaf, lobster and fish heads and bones, and any accumulated juices. Add just enough water to cover the solids, about 6½ cups. Bring to a boil, stir in the saffron, then reduce the heat to low. Simmer for 20 minutes, skimming any foam from the surface. Strain through a sieve into a medium saucepan and keep warm over low heat.

Heat the remaining 2 teaspoons oil in a very large Dutch oven over medium-high heat. Add the rice and cook, stirring, until toasted, 1 to 2 minutes. Stir in the hot seafood stock and 1 tablespoon salt and bring to a boil. Reduce the heat to low and simmer until the rice is just tender, 10 to 20 minutes.

Nestle the lobster claws, knuckles, and tail halves and fish fillets in the rice. Cover and cook until the lobster and fish just lose their translucence on the outside, about 3 minutes. Scatter the mussels in a single layer on top and cover. Cook just until the mussels open and the fish and lobster are just cooked through, about 5 minutes. Gently fold in the vinegar and parsley and serve immediately.

*Lentejas Estofadas*

# LENTILS WITH PORK BELLY AND YUKON GOLD POTATOES

SERVES 4 TO 6 AS A MAIN DISH
OR 8 TO 10 AS A SMALL PLATE

At its core, this combination represents the survival dishes from the Spanish civil war. Traditionally, cheap and filling ingredients were simply boiled together for sustenance. But the Spanish always had good taste—you can't really go wrong with pork, beans, and potatoes. I hope I've made the trio even better by stirring in pimentón at the end. Its subtle smokiness brought a needed complexity to the luscious pork and beans.

1 pound boneless, skinless pork belly, cut into 1-inch cubes

Kosher salt and freshly ground black pepper

1 small green bell pepper, stemmed, seeded, and finely chopped (¾ cup)

1 small onion, finely chopped (½ cup)

3 carrots, peeled and finely chopped (1 cup)

1 garlic clove, minced

¼ cup canned crushed San Marzano tomatoes

1 fresh or dried bay leaf

1¼ cups black beluga or French Le Puy lentils, rinsed well and drained

2 medium Yukon gold potatoes, peeled, quartered lengthwise, and cut into ½-inch slices crosswise (2 cups)

1 teaspoon pimentón (sweet smoked paprika)

HEAT A LARGE DUTCH OVEN OVER MEDIUM-HIGH heat. Sprinkle the pork belly with 1 teaspoon salt and season with pepper. Add to the Dutch oven in a single layer and sear, turning the pieces to evenly brown, about 10 minutes. Move the pork to one side of the Dutch oven. Reduce the heat to medium. Add the pepper, onion, and carrots. Cook, stirring occasionally, until soft, about 10 minutes. Add the garlic and cook, stirring, until fragrant, about 15 seconds. Add the crushed tomatoes and cook, stirring often, until all the liquid evaporates and the tomatoes begin to caramelize, about 5 minutes. Add the bay leaf and 4 cups water. Bring to a boil, then reduce the heat to low and simmer for 40 minutes.

Stir in the lentils and 1½ teaspoons salt. Simmer for 20 minutes. If the mixture begins to dry out, add more water. Stir in the potatoes and simmer until the potatoes and lentils are tender, about 10 minutes. Stir in the pimentón. Taste and add more salt and pepper if you'd like. Serve hot.

The lentils can be cooled completely and refrigerated for up to 3 days. Reheat gently on the stovetop, adding more water if needed.

*Potaje de Garbanzos*

# STEWED CHICKPEAS WITH COLLARDS AND SALT PORK

SERVES 4 TO 6 AS A MAIN DISH
OR 8 TO 10 AS A SMALL PLATE

When I stumbled across this rustic Spanish soup, I had déjà vu. The technique matches that of the collard greens my mom and grandma cooked when I was growing up in South Carolina. Essentially, both the garbanzos and the greens go low and slow with salt pork and ham hocks. I decided to fuse the Spanish and South Carolina dishes by seasoning with pimentón and sherry vinegar and starting with collard greens. I've also introduced tomatoes to the mix. Along with onion and garlic, their sweetness counters the saltiness of the meat while melding into a comforting blend.

COVER THE GARBANZOS WITH COLD WATER BY 4 inches in a large bowl. Cover and refrigerate overnight.

Wash the collards well, then stack 5 or 6 leaves. Cut out the stems and central ribs, slicing along the sides to form a "V." Discard the stems. Roll up the leaves and cut crosswise to form 1-inch-wide ribbons.

Cook the salt pork in a large saucepot over medium heat until the fat renders, about 5 minutes. Add the onion and cook, stirring occasionally, until soft, about 10 minutes. Add the garlic and cook, stirring, until fragrant, about 15 seconds. Add the tomatoes and cook, stirring occasionally, until most of the liquid has evaporated, about 5 minutes. Stir in the bay leaf and pimentón.

Drain the garbanzos and stir into the pot, then add the ham hock and 8 cups water. Bring to a boil over high heat, then stir in the collards and 1 teaspoon salt. Bring back to a boil, reduce the heat to low, and simmer until the garbanzos and ham hock meat are tender, 1½ to 2 hours.

Remove the ham hock. When cool enough to handle, pull off the meat and return to the pot. Discard the bones and cartilage. Stir in the vinegar. Taste and add more salt if you think it needs it. Serve hot.

The stew can be cooled and refrigerated in airtight containers for up 3 days. Reheat gently on the stovetop.

1 pound dried garbanzo beans (chickpeas)

1½ pounds collard greens

6 ounces salt pork, cut into ½-inch cubes

2 large onions, finely chopped (2 cups)

2 garlic cloves, minced

1 cup canned crushed San Marzano tomatoes

1 fresh or dried bay leaf

1 teaspoon pimentón (smoked sweet paprika)

1 ham hock

Kosher salt

2 teaspoons sherry vinegar

*Fabada Asturiana*

# ASTURIAN BEAN AND SAUSAGE STEW

⚶

SERVES 6 TO 8 AS A MAIN DISH
OR 10 TO 12 AS A SMALL PLATE

A few Novembers ago, I had the best fabada asturiana ever. Granted, it was in Asturias, home of this dish. And it did start with fresh Asturian fabe beans, which you can't buy stateside. This is my attempt to reach that level of perfection using dried beans. The products closest to the originals are the bean company Rancho Gordo's cassoulet or yellow-eyed beans. And the best sausages are either homemade (see pages 125 to 130) or ordered through La Tienda or Despaña. When you're making a dish so deeply rooted in a particular region, your best bet is to start with ingredients similar to what's used there. While I can't dictate when you serve your meals, I can advise you to dish this up for lunch all alone or with a simple green salad. You'll need the rest of the day to settle after eating this filling blend of beans and sausage. A glass of red wine or Asturian cider certainly helps, too.

1 pound dried fabes Asturianas, or other white beans

2 cups Chicken Stock (page 136) or store-bought unsalted chicken stock

3 ounces salt pork

2 fresh Chorizo links (page 126) or store-bought

2 fresh Morcilla de Burgos (blood sausage with rice) links (page 130) or store-bought

3 tablespoons unsalted butter

4 tablespoons extra-virgin olive oil, divided

¼ teaspoon saffron

Kosher salt

½ medium onion, very finely chopped

½ teaspoon pimentón (smoked sweet paprika)

COVER THE BEANS WITH COLD WATER BY 2 inches in a large bowl. Cover with plastic wrap and refrigerate overnight.

Drain the beans and place in a large saucepot. Add the chicken stock, then add just enough water to cover the beans, 1 to 2 cups. Nestle the salt pork, chorizo, and morcillas in the beans, then add the butter and 2 tablespoons oil. Bring to a boil over high heat, then reduce the heat to low and simmer for 20 minutes. In the beginning, you can stir everything together with a spoon, but as the beans cook, occasionally pick the pot up and swirl it instead. Stirring will break the beans once they soften. Swirl in the saffron and ½ teaspoon salt.

Meanwhile, heat the remaining 2 tablespoons oil in a small skillet over medium-low heat. Add the onion and pimentón. Cook, stirring often, until everything is caramelized, about 15 minutes. Be careful not to burn the pimentón. Scrape into the pot with the beans and simmer for another 20 minutes.

Taste the beans to see if they are done. If not, continue simmering until they are tender all the way through, probably another 20 minutes or so. If the liquid level drops below the beans, add water. The whole stew can be cooled at this point and refrigerated for up to 3 days.

When ready to serve, transfer the salt pork and sausages to a cutting board. Cut into bite-size pieces, then return to the pot. Taste and add more salt if you think it needs it. Serve hot.

*Monjetes*

# GARLICKY SAUTÉED WHITE BEANS

MAKES 3 CUPS; SERVES 4 AS A MAIN DISH
OR 6 AS A SMALL PLATE

A cool thing happens when well-dried freshly cooked beans hit hot oil and sear hard. Their skins blister into a crackly delicate shell and the insides become extra tender and creamy. Monjetes are as good as they sound: a wonder of texture with toasty garlic and fresh parsley. This Catalonian bean dish is addictive on its own with a swipe of allioli in each bite and turns into a full meal with a side of sausages, such as Butifarra (page 125).

4 tablespoons plus 2 teaspoons blended oil, divided

3 cups Basic White Beans, very well drained, divided

1½ packed teaspoons minced garlic, divided

Kosher salt

1 teaspoon extra-virgin olive oil

1 teaspoon packed, minced fresh flat-leaf parsley leaves

Aliolli (page 182) for serving

HEAT 2 TABLESPOONS BLENDED OIL IN A VERY large cast-iron or other heavy skillet over high heat until just smoking. Add half of the beans and shake the pan to get them in an even layer. Don't touch them. Let sit so they turn golden brown on the undersides. Once they're brown, shake the pan again to toss them. Continue cooking, tossing occasionally, until evenly golden brown and crusty, 3 to 4 minutes total. Transfer to a dish. Repeat with another 2 tablespoons blended oil and the remaining beans, transferring them to the same dish.

Add the remaining 2 teaspoons blended oil and the garlic to the skillet. Cook, stirring, until golden brown and fragrant, about 1 minute. Return the beans to the pan, toss well, season with ½ teaspoon salt, and toss again. Drizzle with the olive oil and sprinkle with the parsley and toss again. Taste and add more salt if you'd like.

Immediately transfer to a serving dish and serve right away with the allioli.

## BASIC WHITE BEANS

MAKES 7 CUPS (2½ POUNDS)

In some cases, you can swap canned beans for freshly cooked. Not so with Monjetes. You must start with these tender yet toothsome beans; canned ones turn to a greasy mush. Besides, it's handy to have a basic bean recipe for anything from soups and stews to salads and starters. This is best made with the Ayacote Blanco beans from Rancho Gordo.

1 pound great Northern white beans or navy beans, broken beans discarded

1 smoked ham hock

½ small yellow onion

4 large garlic cloves, peeled

1 fresh or dried bay leaf

⅛ teaspoon whole black peppercorns

COVER BEANS WITH COLD WATER BY 3 INCHES IN a large bowl. Cover with plastic wrap and refrigerate overnight.

Drain the beans well and transfer to a stockpot.

Wrap the ham hock, onion, garlic, bay leaf, and peppercorns in a large piece of cheesecloth and tie with kitchen string. Transfer to the pot with the beans and add enough cold water to cover by 2 inches.

Bring to a simmer over high heat, then reduce the heat to low to maintain a bare simmer. Simmer until the beans are tender but still holding their shape, about 1 hour. Remove from the heat and strain through a colander.

If you want to make the beans ahead, cool to room temperature in the liquid, pour off some of the liquid, cover, and refrigerate for up to 1 week. Discard the sachet of aromatics.

# BRUNCH AND LUNCH

*Carajillo de Brandy*
*con Nata Montada*

# SPANISH COFFEE WITH ORANGE WHIPPED CREAM

**SERVES 8**

Breakfast in Spain means little more than coffee. Here's how you can order it:

**Café con Leche:** 50/50 espresso and hot milk

**Cortado:** 75/25 espresso with a dash of steamed milk

**Carajillo:** espresso with a shot of rum, whiskey, anisette, or your favorite liqueur

**Trifasico:** cortado with a shot

Those last two boozy options are popular among workers who need just a little something to keep them warm and get them going for work. And they're the inspiration for our take on Spanish coffee. We fused that concept with that of Irish coffee when we were coming up with drinks for Cúrate's brunch menu. To give it a Spanish twist, we swapped brandy for whiskey. Orange turned out to be a natural match, so it found its way into the whipped cream top.

1 cup heavy cream

½ cup strained fresh orange juice, orange rinds reserved

2 tablespoons confectioners' sugar

8 (2-ounce) shots hot espresso

6 ounces Spanish brandy, preferably Gran Duque de Alba

3 tablespoons turbinado sugar

1 coffee bean

WHISK THE CREAM, JUICE, AND CONFECTIONers' sugar with an electric mixer on medium speed in a large bowl until soft peaks form.

Stir the espresso, brandy, and turbinado sugar in a 1-pint liquid measuring cup or bowl with a spout until the sugar dissolves. Divide among martini glasses. Dollop the orange whipped cream on top, then zest the reserved orange rinds and the coffee bean over the cream. Serve immediately.

*Huevos con Puntilla*

# THE **BEST** **FRIED EGG EVER**

Félix's mom—and, therefore, Félix—makes the best fried eggs ever. Huevos con Puntilla means "eggs with lace" and that's exactly how these eggs look. The beautiful golden brown crispy tendrils that form around the egg when it is fried in ripping-hot oil are as delicate and beautiful as lace. Since the eggs cook so quickly, the edges become potato chip crunchy, the whites moist, and the yolk runny and rich as hollandaise. Here's how to do it:

- Use a small nonstick pan to save yourself from sticking worries. A nonstick silicone spatula, too (the flat pancake-flipping kind, not the scraping-the-bowl one). A metal spatula might stick to the egg and scratch your pan. And a rubber spatula that can't withstand really high heat might warp.

- Turn on the exhaust fan over your stove or open windows if you don't have a hood.

- Fill the pan with a high-heat oil, like canola, sunflower, or peanut; a ½ inch is good here. This is a "fried" egg in that it's really, truly fried, so don't skimp on the oil.

- Get the oil really hot. Wisps of smoke should start to rise. The reason we're doing it that hot is because the egg yolk has to be runny and the white has to be crispy. If the oil's not hot enough, you're going to overcook the egg yolk by the time the white sets. Eggs like to get cooked fast. It's a lot of oil, but if it's at the right temperature—yes, as in, really hot—the egg isn't going to absorb much of it at all.

- Carefully and quickly crack an egg into the pan. Watch out! The egg will sizzle and possibly pop. Once the egg goes in the oil, sprinkle the yolk with kosher salt and start spooning the surrounding oil on top with the flat of the spatula. The white will bubble up and cover the yolk. The sides and bottom of the egg will turn golden brown around the sides and on the bottom. This whole process takes less than a minute. Lift the egg out with the spatula and let excess oil drip off. Serve immediately.

- Keep making the eggs, one at a time. Be sure to heat the oil well before adding the next egg.

- When you're all done, turn off the fire and eat your own egg right away.

- After the oil cools to room temperature, strain it and reuse it until it no longer has that clear golden color.

## HUEVOS CON PISTO MANCHEGO

MAKE THE PISTO MANCHEGO (PAGE 154) AND DIVVY hot mounds among serving plates. Top each with a fried egg. Cut up the egg and let the yolk run into the vegetables. Alternatively, spread the Pisto Manchego in a 10-inch ovenproof skillet. Make 4 to 6 divots in the Pisto Manchego and fill each one with a raw egg. Broil until the eggs are cooked through.

*Huevos Rotos*

# FRIED EGGS OVER POTATO CHIPS AND SERRANO HAM

**SERVES 4**

There's nothing not to like about huevos rotos, a hearty breakfast or lunch dish found all over Spain. Potato slices fry until crisp around the edges, but stay tender and sweet in the centers, then get tossed with Serrano ham for a porky saltiness. The savory pile gets topped with crackly fried eggs, which are cut all over the mix so the yolk sauces everything.

1 medium Idaho potato (12 ounces), peeled, divided

Blended oil, for frying

Kosher salt

4 ounces very thinly sliced Serrano ham, torn into bite-size pieces

4 large eggs, divided

USE A MANDOLINE TO SLICE THE POTATO INTO potato-chip-thin slices. If you don't have a mandoline, you can use the slicing attachment on a food processor or a very sharp knife and impeccable knife skills. Toss with just enough oil to prevent the slices from sticking to one another.

Fill a large, deep skillet with oil to a depth of ½ inch. Heat over high heat until hot. Add just enough potatoes to fit in a single layer and cook, carefully tossing and turning, until just golden, about 1 minute. The edges will be browned and crisp, but the centers should be a bit soft. Use a slotted spoon to transfer the fried potatoes to a large colander. Repeat with the remaining potatoes. Sprinkle with salt in the colander and toss to evenly distribute the salt and shake off excess oil. Toss in the ham, then divide among serving plates.

When the oil is hot again, carefully add an egg. Fry, spooning the hot oil on top, until browned around the edges and the white is cooked through. Use a rubber spatula to carefully transfer to the top of a potato pile. Repeat with the remaining eggs. Serve hot, cutting up the egg and letting the yolk run all over the chips and ham.

*Arroz a la Cubana*

# GARLIC RICE WITH TOMATO SAUCE AND FRIED EGG AND BANANA

## SERVES 4

When Cuba was a Spanish colony, it exported parts of its culture to Spain. Arroz a la cubana is a dish that found its way from Cuba onto Spanish plates. In Spain, it doesn't often have the fried banana that's common in the Latin American versions. I think the sweetness from the banana makes the dish, so I always add it. It's a surprising counterpoint to the garlicky rice, saucy tomatoes, and runny egg. And I'm adding my own Southern twist by using bacon and Anson Mills heirloom Carolina Gold rice. Its perfume is intoxicating in the morning. This dish is delicious even without those lovely grains. Any type of rice will work; you can even skip the rice-cooking step and use leftover rice from takeout. Félix and I like to leisurely cook this together on Sunday mornings when we (try to!) take the day off to relax. Ideally, the tomato sauce and rice simmer at the same time, then the rice and banana fry simultaneously. While all those components are doled onto plates, the eggs should be fried and slipped on top right before serving. It's fun to tag-team the process with family or friends so that everyone can sit down and eat the meal hot all together.

2 cups Carolina Gold rice, preferably Anson Mills

2 fresh or dried bay leaves

10 garlic cloves, peeled and sliced, divided

2 slices bacon, cut into ½-inch pieces

¼ cup finely chopped onion

2 cups canned crushed San Marzano tomatoes

Kosher salt

2 tablespoons blended oil, divided

2 bananas, halved lengthwise

4 Best Fried Eggs Ever (page 210)

BRING THE RICE, BAY LEAVES, 2 GARLIC CLOVES, and 1½ cups water to a boil in a large saucepan, stirring occasionally. Cover, reduce the heat to low, and simmer until the rice is tender and the water absorbed, about 20 minutes. Let stand 5 minutes, then uncover and fluff with a fork. Discard the bay leaves.

While the rice cooks, cook the bacon in a large saucepan over medium heat, stirring occasionally, until the fat renders and the bacon is golden brown, about 4 minutes. Add 4 garlic cloves and stir until golden but not dark brown, about 2 minutes. Add the onion, reduce the heat to medium-low and cook, stirring and scraping up the browned bits, until the onions are soft, about 2 minutes. Add the tomatoes and ¼ teaspoon salt. Raise the heat to high to bring to a boil, then reduce the heat to medium-low to simmer until the mixture thickens, about 3 minutes. Keep warm over low heat.

Heat 1 tablespoon oil in a large cast-iron or nonstick skillet over medium-high heat. Add the remaining 4 garlic cloves and cook, stirring, until golden, about 1 minute. Add the rice and cook, stirring to separate the grains and heat through, about 2 minutes. Divide among 4 serving plates and scrape the skillet clean.

Heat the remaining tablespoon oil in the skillet. Add the bananas and cook, turning once, until nicely browned, about 1 minute per side. Divide among the serving plates. Spoon the warm tomato sauce alongside the rice and top with a fried egg. Serve immediately, cutting the egg up and mixing the yolk with the tomato sauce and rice.

*Torrijas*

# SPANISH FRENCH TOAST

### SERVES 8

In Madrid, torrijas are traditionally reserved for Easter as a post-Lenten dessert and traditionally made with leftover baguettes. I like to use brioche or other egg breads, such as challah, for an even richer dessert. The custard-soaked egg bread develops a delicate lushness that resembles bread pudding. I like to take it even one step further by bruléeing sugar on top for a crunchy crust. It actually tempers the cinnamon custard's sweetness because the burnt sugar takes on a bitter-sweet edge. This dessert-for-brunch dish beats any typical French toast.

**1 cup heavy cream**

**1 cup half-and-half**

**Zest of 1 lemon, removed in strips with a vegetable peeler**

**Zest of 1 orange, removed in strips with a vegetable peeler**

**1 cinnamon stick**

**4 large eggs, room temperature**

**¼ cup plus 8 teaspoons granulated sugar**

**1 (12-ounce) loaf brioche, ends trimmed, loaf cut in 8 (1-inch-thick) slices**

**Clarified butter, for cooking**

BRING THE CREAM, HALF-AND-HALF, LEMON zest, orange zest, and cinnamon to a simmer in a medium saucepan over medium heat. While the mixture heats, whisk the eggs and ¼ cup sugar in a large bowl. Slowly add the hot liquid to the egg mixture in a steady stream, whisking constantly.

Lay the brioche slices in a single layer in glass or ceramic baking dishes. Slowly and evenly pour the egg-cream mixture over the bread, scattering the zest and cinnamon evenly over the bread. Cover tightly with plastic wrap and refrigerate overnight.

Uncover the soaked brioche and discard the zest and cinnamon. Heat a thin sheen of clarified butter in a large nonstick skillet over medium heat. Add a single layer of soaked brioche slices and cook, turning once, until evenly browned on both sides and cooked through, about 6 minutes. Transfer to a half-sheet pan. Repeat with the remaining brioche slices, coating the skillet with clarified butter between batches. If the brioche browns before the center is heated through, reduce the heat.

Sprinkle a teaspoon of sugar evenly on top of each cooked slice. Using a kitchen blowtorch, caramelize the sugar on each piece of brioche as you would crème brulée. Serve immediately.

*Empanada Gallega*

# SAVORY TOMATO, TUNA, AND BELL PEPPER TART

### ⚓

MAKES ONE 12-INCH TART;
SERVES 6 TO 8 AS A MAIN COURSE
OR 12 TO 16 AS A SMALL PLATE

At tapas bars all over Spain, cold wedges of this tart are served with chilled lager. The secret to the tart's richness is using the oil from the filling's sofrito in the dough. Yes, it is a lot of oil, but it infuses the dough with sweetness and keeps it tender. It also makes the dough easy to roll and shape. You don't even have to worry about crimping the edges prettily. The golden hue from baking compensates for any imperfections.

This tart makes for an impressive make-ahead lunch. You want to serve it at room temperature, not hot, and it tastes even richer after it's sat in the refrigerator overnight. Just bring it back to room temperature before serving with a salad or Gazpacho (page 39).

½ cup extra-virgin olive oil, plus more if needed

1 large onion, very thinly sliced

1 large red bell pepper, stemmed, seeded, and very thinly sliced

1 tablespoon minced garlic

1 cup canned crushed San Marzano tomatoes

1 (6-ounce) jar tuna packed in olive oil, drained and shredded (1 cup)

2 tablespoons thinly sliced pitted Kalamata olives

Kosher salt

3 cups all-purpose flour

2¼ teaspoons instant yeast

2 large eggs, divided

1 tablespoon heavy cream

To make the filling, start by making the sofrito. Combine the oil and onion in a large skillet and cook over medium heat, stirring occasionally, until the onion is glassy, about 10 minutes. Add the bell pepper and garlic and cook, stirring occasionally, until all the vegetables are very soft, about 20 minutes. If the vegetables start to brown, lower the heat. Set a fine-mesh sieve over a liquid measuring cup and pour the vegetables into the strainer. Let sit until the oil and juices drain out, then return the vegetables to the pan and reserve the oil.

Add the tomatoes to the onion mixture and cook over medium heat, stirring occasionally, until most of the liquid has evaporated, but the mixture isn't dry, about 10 minutes. Stir in the tuna, olives, and 1½ teaspoons salt. Taste and add more salt if necessary. Transfer to an airtight container and refrigerate until cold, at least 2 hours and up to overnight.

To make the dough, see if you have ¾ cup sofrito oil in your measuring cup. If not, add enough olive oil to make up the difference. Pulse the flour, yeast, and 2¼ teaspoons salt in a food processor until well-mixed. Add the sofrito oil and ½ cup water. Process until the dough comes together. Turn the dough out onto a work surface, knead a couple of times, then roll it into a ball. Place in a bowl, cover with plastic wrap, and let stand at room temperature for 2 hours.

Meanwhile, fill a small bowl with ice and water. Bring a small saucepan of water to a boil. Add 1 egg and cook for 12 minutes. Transfer to the ice bath. When cool, peel and dice. Beat the remaining egg with the cream in a small bowl.

Preheat the oven to 375°F.

Divide the dough in half and roll each on a sheet of parchment paper into a 13-inch round (⅛-inch thick). Slide one round of dough on the parchment onto a rimless cookie sheet. Spread the sofrito filling evenly over the dough, leaving a ¾-inch rim. Sprinkle the hard-boiled egg

*(Continued)*

evenly on top. Pat the egg into the filling to make sure there are no air pockets in the filling. Lift the other dough round using the parchment paper and flip it over the filling, aligning its edges with the bottom dough. Peel off the top parchment. Press the edges together, then seal by holding a section of the top and bottom edges together between your thumb and forefinger and folding it over so the bottom comes up over the top. Press the folded-over edge to seal. Repeat around the rest of the rim.

Brush the beaten egg all over the top of the empanada. Use a sharp knife to cut a 1-inch X in the center of the empanada, then cut three 1-inch long air vents around the center. Firmly press down the dough to remove any air pockets. Cut the air vents open again if needed.

Bake until golden brown, 45 minutes to 1 hour. Cool on the pan on a wire rack to serve warm or room temperature.

A completely cooled empanada can be covered with plastic wrap and refrigerated overnight. Let stand at room temperature to take the chill off before serving.

*Bocadillos*

# SANDWICHES

Fried Squid Sandwich (p. 223)

Sausage Sandwich
with Onions and Piquillos

*Bocadillo Catalán*

## SAUSAGE SANDWICHES WITH **ONIONS** AND **PIQUILLOS**

MAKES 4

Hailing from the home of butifarra sausage, this Catalonian specialty is the irresistible marriage of salty pork and sweet peppers and onions.

SEAR 4 BUTIFARRA SAUSAGES (PAGE 125) IN A cast-iron skillet over low heat until nicely browned and cooked through. At the same time, get the vegetables ready. The ideal scenario is to use the Confit Piquillo Peppers (page 173). If you don't have those on hand, pat 8 piquillo peppers very dry, then sear them in a tablespoon of olive oil in a hot skillet. Transfer the piquillos to a plate, add another tablespoon oil to the pan, and stir in a very thinly sliced large onion and season with salt. Cook until totally soft. If the onion starts to get a little too dark, add a little water to the pan. That actually helps it to appear like caramelized onions in a shorter amount of time. Split a baguette to open sandwich-style and cut in 4 even pieces or cut 8 slices from a rustic country loaf. Toast in a toaster oven or broiler, then smear Allioli (page 182) on the top halves. Spread the caramelized onions on the bottom halves and top each with 2 peppers. Cut the sausages in half lengthwise, press on top of the piquillos, and sandwich with the top halves.

If you want, you can grill the sausage over low heat and grill the bread alongside instead.

## SPANISH BLT

I'm an all-American girl at heart with an abiding love of BLTs. I didn't think the original could get any better until I shoved a slice of tortilla in there and smeared the bread with olive oil mayo.

THIS SANDWICH IS A PRETTY BASIC ONE MADE BY toasting whole-grain sandwich bread, spreading the slices with Arbequina Olive Oil Mayonnaise (page 49) then sandwiching in thick slices of Tortilla Española (page 25) tomato slices, lettuce leaves, and crisped thick-cut bacon. That's it: a BLT with tortilla.

*Bocata de Calamares*

## FRIED SQUID SANDWICH

MAKES 4

In Madrid, storefront windows display the city's signature sandwiches. When I first tasted one, it reminded me of a Southern po' boy. Depending on my mood, I'll stick to Madrid's crusty baguette-style sandwiches or swap in sweet and soft potato rolls for a taste of New Orleans.

PREP A POUND OF SQUID BY CUTTING THE BODIES in ¼-inch rings and the tentacles in half, then soaking in whole milk overnight in the fridge. Mix ¾ cup garbanzo bean (chickpea) flour with ¼ cup all-purpose flour in a large bowl. Drain the squid and toss in the flour mixture until well-coated. Fill a cast-iron skillet with canola oil to ½-inch depth and heat over high heat until very hot. Fry the squid in batches, adding only as much as can fit in a single layer without crowding. Shake any excess flour off first and turn to evenly brown. These cook really quickly, in a minute or two. As soon as they come out of the oil, drain on paper towels and sprinkle with salt and pepper. Finish by zesting a bit of lemon zest over the top. Sandwich between toasted split baguette or potato rolls spread with Arbequina Olive Oil Mayonnaise (page 49).

## PAN con TOMATE SANDWICHES

The first time I ever had a pan con tomate sandwich was during an all-day date with Félix. He packed two for us—they were the road-trip sandwiches of his childhood—and when I dug into mine hours after we'd left that morning, I was overwhelmed. I decided it was the best sandwich I'd ever had. It holds up well from morning to lunch, with its crusty bread and charcuterie. Of course, it's really good the second after you assemble it, too.

**M**AKE PAN CON TOMATE (PAGE 22) THEN SANDwich 2 pieces with sliced charcuterie, like chorizo or Serrano ham, and then you can add sliced Manchego cheese. It's a great picnic sandwich or any type of to-go sandwich because it holds up really well.

*Bocadillo de Atún*

## TUNA SANDWICH

Yes, this is a sandwich made mainly with canned products. But that's the beauty of Spanish cuisine. So many of its packaged goods are actually whole foods, and delicious ones at that. When I'm wiped after a long day at work, I turn to this sandwich. Not only because it's so easy but also because I love its stack of juicy vegetables, meaty tuna and egg, and creamy mayonnaise.

**T**HIS IS A GREAT TUNA SANDWICH. HERE ARE THE components: toasted baguette, Arbequina Olive Oil Mayonnaise (page 49) canned Navarra white asparagus, drained piquillo peppers, tuna jarred in olive oil, and sliced hard-boiled egg. Sounds strange, but it is delicious if you use high-quality jarred asparagus, peppers, and tuna. For 4 sandwiches, you'll need 1 baguette cut in quarters and split, 6 halved asparagus spears, 8 piquillos, a 6- to 7-ounce jar tuna, and as much mayonnaise as you want.

Tuna Sandwich

*Pepito de Ternera*

# STEAK, GREEN PEPPER, AND BLUE CHEESE SANDWICH

MAKES 4

When I first saw this sandwich in Spain, I immediately thought of Philly cheesesteak. It had steak piled with caramelized peppers and onions and I thought, "I bet blue cheese would be great on that." Turns out I was right. The savory sharpness of blue cheese tempers the sweetness of caramelized onion and pepper while standing up to hearty steak.

1 pound skirt steak

Kosher salt and freshly ground black pepper

Extra-virgin olive oil

½ large onion, thinly sliced

1 green bell pepper, stemmed, seeded, and thinly sliced

1 (12- to 14-inch) demi-baguette

1 ounce blue cheese, such as Valdeón, crumbled (¼ cup)

**H**EAT A LARGE CAST-IRON SKILLET OVER HIGH heat. Sprinkle 1 teaspoon salt all over the steak, then season with pepper. Add enough oil to lightly coat the bottom of the skillet. When it's almost smoking, add the steak. Cook, turning once, until nicely seared, about 3 minutes per side for medium-rare. Transfer to a cutting board. Reduce the heat to low. If the pan is dry, add enough oil to coat the bottom, then add the onion and pepper. Cook, stirring occasionally, until very soft, about 12 minutes. Season with ½ teaspoon salt.

While the vegetables cook, preheat the oven to broil, on a low broil setting if you have it.

Trim the ends of the baguette, then cut in half lengthwise to create a top and bottom for the sandwiches. Brush the cut sides with olive oil and place on a foil-lined half-sheet pan. Broil until golden, 1 to 3 minutes.

Thinly slice the steak across the grain and layer it on the bottom half of the baguette. Top with the onion and pepper, then sprinkle with the cheese. Return to the broiler and heat just until the cheese melts, 1 to 2 minutes. Sandwich with the top half of the baguette and cut in quarters. Serve immediately.

# DESSERTS

*Tarta de Santiago*

# ALMOND CAKE WITH CREAM SHERRY AND BRANDY

### MAKES ONE 9-INCH CAKE

The relics of Saint James are believed to be buried in Galicia's Cathedral of Santiago de Compostela. Pilgrims from around the world who trek the Camino de Santiago end up at the site. Though the origins of Santiago's eponymous cake aren't clear, its current popularity is evident in the streets of Galicia. Pastry shops for miles around the cathedral, and even beyond Galicia's borders, sell rich almond cakes sugar-emblazoned with the cross of Saint James. (You can find a stencil online to print and cut out to dust the top with confectioner's sugar.) While many bakers make low, tart-like cakes, I prefer a taller one. And I like to soak it with cream sherry and brandy. For a more traditional take, you can skip that final step. This cake is sweet enough for dessert, but also works well with tea in the afternoon or for brunch.

8 tablespoons unsalted butter, melted and cooled, plus more for the pan

2⅓ cups sliced skin-on almonds, divided

¼ cup plus 1 table-spoon all-purpose flour

1 teaspoon kosher salt

Zest of ½ lemon

6 large egg yolks, room temperature

1 cup plus 2 tablespoons granulated sugar

3 large egg whites, room temperature

2 tablespoons cream sherry

3 tablespoons brandy

Confectioners' sugar, for decorating

PREHEAT THE OVEN TO 325°F. BUTTER A 9-INCH-round (2-inch-deep) cake pan, line the bottom with parchment paper, and butter again.

Spread ⅓ cup almonds on a half-sheet pan and bake until golden brown, about 10 minutes. Cool completely on the pan, then spread in an even layer on the bottom of the prepared cake pan.

Meanwhile, grind the remaining 2 cups almonds in a food processor until very finely ground. Transfer to a large bowl and whisk in the flour, salt, and lemon zest. Reserve.

Beat the egg yolks, ¾ cup granulated sugar, and 2 tablespoons hot water with the whisk attachment of an electric mixer on medium-high speed until tripled in volume, light, and airy, about 5 minutes. With the machine running, slowly pour in the melted butter in a steady stream. Remove from the mixer and very gently fold in the almond flour mixture. Be careful not to overmix; mix it just until incorporated and reserve.

Beat the egg whites with a clean whisk attachment in a clean bowl with an electric mixer on medium speed until soft peaks form. With the machine running, add ¼ cup sugar in a steady stream. Continue to beat until stiff peaks form. Gently fold the whipped whites into the egg yolk mixture. Be sure not to deflate the mixture. Gently and carefully dollop the batter over the almonds in the cake pan, then smooth the top.

Bake until a cake tester inserted in the center comes out clean, 40 to 50 minutes.

While the cake bakes, heat the sherry and remaining 2 tablespoons sugar in a small saucepan over medium heat, stirring until the sugar dissolves. Remove from the heat and stir in the brandy.

When the cake is done, cool it in the pan on a wire rack for 5 minutes. With a pastry brush, brush half of the syrup on top of the cake. Cool completely in the pan on the rack. Invert the cake onto a serving plate and brush the remaining syrup on top. Cover tightly with plastic wrap and let stand overnight.

When ready to serve, place the stencil of the cross of Saint James (Santiago cross) on top of the cake and dust around it with a nice layer of confectioner's sugar. Remove the stencil and serve.

*Brazo de Gitano*

# WHITE CHOCOLATE SAFFRON ROULADE

SERVES 8 TO 12

Brazo de Gitano translates to "arm of a gypsy," possibly because of its long shape. Like a French roulade or Swiss roll, this dessert is a spiral of tender cake and filling. All over Spain, the fillings range from jams to caramel to chocolate to flavored cream. I thought sugary white chocolate and earthy saffron could work well in a pastry cream filling. But it took me a little while to strike the right balance because they complement each other but can overpower each other, too.

### WHITE CHOCOLATE SAFFRON PASTRY CREAM

1½ cups whole milk

¼ teaspoon saffron threads

4 large egg yolks

⅓ cup all-purpose flour

½ cup plus 1 tablespoon granulated sugar, divided

2½ ounces white chocolate, finely chopped

1¼ cups heavy cream

### CAKE

Nonstick cooking spray

⅔ cup cake flour

2½ tablespoons cornstarch

3 large egg yolks

2 large eggs

½ cup plus 1 tablespoon superfine sugar, divided

¼ teaspoon salt

2 large egg whites

¼ teaspoon cream of tartar

Confectioners' sugar, for dusting

TO MAKE THE PASTRY CREAM, BRING THE MILK and saffron to a boil in a large saucepan. While the milk heats, whisk the egg yolks, all-purpose flour, and ½ cup granulated sugar in a medium bowl. Continue whisking while adding the hot milk in a slow, steady stream. Return the mixture to the saucepan and cook over medium heat, whisking continuously, until the mixture comes to a boil and thickens, about 5 minutes. Boil the mixture, whisking continuously, for 1 minute. The mixture should be a very thick paste so that when mixed with whipped cream it won't become too thin and run out of the rolled cake. If it isn't very thick, keep cooking and whisking.

Press through a fine-mesh sieve into a large bowl and add the chocolate. Stir until the chocolate melts and the mixture is smooth. Press a sheet of plastic wrap directly against the surface and refrigerate until cold.

While the pastry cream chills, make the cake. Position a rack in the middle of the oven and preheat to 450°F. Coat a half-sheet pan with nonstick cooking spray, line the bottom with parchment paper, and spray again.

Whisk the cake flour and cornstarch in a small bowl. Whisk the egg yolks, whole eggs, and ½ cup superfine sugar with an electric mixer on high speed until thick, fluffy, and tripled in volume, about 5 minutes. Reduce the speed to medium and beat in the salt. Transfer to another large bowl. Clean the mixer bowl and whisk attachment thoroughly.

Sift half the flour mixture over the beaten egg mixture and gently fold in until almost all of the flour has disappeared. Repeat with remaining flour.

Whisk the egg whites with the clean electric mixer on medium speed until foamy. Add the cream of tartar and continue whisking until soft peaks form. With the mixer running, add the remaining 1 tablespoon superfine sugar. Continue beating until stiff peaks form. Gently fold into the other egg mixture until well blended, but try not to deflate the egg whites. Pour the batter into the prepared pan and smooth the surface with an offset spatula.

Bake until barely golden brown on top, 6 to 8 minutes. The cake should spring back when

*(Continued)*

lightly pressed in the center, but be sure to avoid overbaking. The cake is more moist and tender when it's baked just until done.

Run an offset spatula around the edges of the cake if they're stuck to the sides. Center a clean sheet of parchment paper, then a wire rack, over the cake. Wearing oven mitts, hold the rack and pan together and invert. Lift off the pan and peel off the parchment paper stuck to the cake. Dust the surface of the cake with confectioners' sugar. With a long side of the cake facing you, roll it up along with the clean sheet of parchment. Cool completely, in its rolled form with the parchment, on the rack.

When the cake is cool, finish the filling. Whisk the cream with the remaining 1 tablespoon granulated sugar with an electric mixer until stiff peaks form. Add the pastry cream and change to the paddle attachment. Beat on low speed until the pastry cream is incorporated, then gradually raise the speed as needed to fully blend the pastry cream and whipped cream until smooth.

Gently unroll the cake and spread the filling on top using an offset spatula, leaving a ½-inch rim along one long side. With the other long side facing you, roll the cake away from you, gently pressing after each roll and peeling off the parchment as you go. Transfer to a serving plate, cover with plastic wrap, and refrigerate until set, at least 4 hours and up to 2 days. It's best after 1 day.

When ready to serve, uncover and dust with confectioners' sugar before slicing.

*Polvorones*

# MARCONA ALMOND HOLIDAY COOKIES

### MAKES 2 TO 3 DOZEN

The name polvorones derives from the Spanish word polvo, which means "dust." It makes sense because they're so delicate they fall apart in your mouth. Classic recipes call for regular almonds, but I prefer buttery roasted Marcona almonds. What I didn't change though is the use of lard. The Spanish love pork so much, they even use it in their desserts. I tried to swap in butter, but the cookie ends up harder. The lard yields a melt-in-your-mouth crumbly round that still retains a toasty cookie appeal. Just be sure to buy high-quality rendered leaf lard, which comes from the fat that runs along the pig's loin and encases its kidneys.

Polvorones are traditionally baked for Christmas, so we make over 600 to give away to diners on Christmas Eve. The cookies make ideal holiday gifts because they keep well. Just be sure to store them in cookie tins or other hard containers with lids, separating layers with wax paper, because they do crumble easily. You can dust the cookies with confectioner's sugar if you'd like, but they're delicious unadorned.

2½ cups all-purpose flour

1 cup roasted salted Marcona almonds, preferably skin on

1¼ cups lard (7¾ ounces), chilled and cut into chunks

1¼ cups packed confectioners' sugar

1 tablespoon lemon zest

1 tablespoon fennel seeds

PREHEAT THE OVEN TO 350°F.

Spread the flour on a half-sheet pan. Place in the oven and bake, stirring once or twice, until lightly toasted and fragrant, about 15 minutes. It'll smell toasty, but not color at all. Cool completely on the pan on a wire rack.

Process the almonds in a food processor until finely ground, scraping the bowl occasionally. Beat the lard and confectioners' sugar in a large bowl with an electric mixer on low speed until well-blended. Once the sugar is completely incorporated into the lard, add the cooled toasted flour, ground almonds, lemon zest, and fennel seeds. Beat on low, scraping the bowl occasionally, until the mixture is completely blended and crumbly with a few larger clumps.

Transfer the clumps and crumbs to a clean work surface. Gather together and press firmly into a 1-inch-thick rectangle. Flatten to ½-inch thickness by rolling with a rolling pan or patting with your hands. Cut into 1½- or 2-inch rounds using a round cookie cutter. Transfer to ungreased cookie sheets by sliding a thin offset spatula or bench scraper under each round and placing on the sheets, spacing 1 inch apart. Press together, flatten, and cut out the scraps.

Bake, 1 sheet at a time, until the cookies are just barely starting to brown on the sides and on the bottom, 15 to 20 minutes. Cool completely on the sheets on wire racks.

The polvorones can be stored in an airtight container at room temperature for up to 1 week.

*Flan de Huevo*

# EGG FLAN

SERVES 8 TO 12

Flan is the classic Spanish dessert found all over the country. This recipe is unadulterated because I love the pure, simple flavor of eggs with milk and sugar. I add just a bit of lemon peel to give the custard more complexity and a bright citrus note.

2½ cups granulated sugar, divided

3 cups whole milk

2 strips lemon zest, removed with a vegetable peeler

⅛ teaspoon salt

6 large eggs

2 large egg yolks

PREHEAT THE OVEN TO 325°F. PLACE A 9- BY 5- BY 4-inch loaf pan inside a 9- by 13-inch baking dish or pan. Bring a large kettle or pot of water to a boil.

Stir 1 cup sugar and 2 tablespoons water in a medium saucepan over medium heat until well combined. Cook without stirring, but brush any sugar crystals off the sides of the pan with a wet pastry brush. Swirl the pan occasionally to caramelize evenly and cook until deep amber in color. Immediately pour into the loaf pan and tilt the pan to evenly coat the bottom and a few inches up the sides.

Bring the milk, lemon zest, salt, and ¾ cup sugar to a simmer in a large saucepan. Meanwhile, whisk the eggs and yolks with the remaining ¾ cup sugar in a large bowl. Continue whisking while adding the hot milk mixture in a slow, steady stream. Strain through a fine-mesh sieve into a 2-quart liquid measuring cup or bowl with a spout. Skim any foam on the surface. Pour into the caramel-lined loaf pan. The mixture will come all the way to the top. Very carefully place the full pan inside the empty baking dish in the oven, then carefully pour the boiling water into the baking dish so that it comes halfway up the sides of the loaf pan.

Bake until just set, but still slightly wobbly in the center, about 1 hour and 5 minutes.

Carefully remove the flan from the water and cool on a wire rack for 30 minutes. Refrigerate uncovered until cold and set, at least 8 hours or up to 3 days.

To unmold, run a sharp knife around the edges. Center a serving plate on top of the pan and carefully and quickly flip the pan and plate together. Lift off the pan and let the caramel run all over the top.

*Crema Catalana*
*con Frutas del Bosque*

---

# BRÛLÉED CUSTARD WITH BERRIES

꙳

### SERVES 8

Throughout Catalonia, restaurants and dessert shops sell shallow dishes of this eggy custard. The oldest institutions burn the sugar on top with a branding iron. As much as I love the original, I also love the tartness that berries add to the cream base. Plus, they look beautiful when peeking through that thin sheet of caramelized sugar. The berries are great, but don't add more than the amounts below. If you toss in more berries than called for in this recipe, the liquid they exude while cooking will mess up your custard as it sets.

You do need shallow ramekins for this. Spanish ones are round, but oblong French crème brûlée dishes would work, too. Finally, the last step may seem counterintuitive: Why chill the custard again after caramelizing the sugar? Trust me, the flavor actually deepens in those 20 minutes. It's worth the wait.

POSITION RACKS IN THE CENTER AND LOWER third of the oven and preheat to 300°F. Arrange 8 shallow (5-ounce) ramekins (4 inches round) in two roasting pans or large baking dishes. Divide the berries among the ramekins in a single layer. Bring a large kettle or pot of water to a boil.

Combine the cream, granulated sugar, and salt in a large saucepan. Scrape the seeds from the vanilla bean and add the seeds and pod. Bring to a boil over medium-high heat, stirring to dissolve the sugar. Remove from the heat.

Meanwhile, whisk the egg yolks in a large bowl. While whisking, add the hot cream mixture in a steady stream. Pour through a fine-mesh sieve into a 1-quart liquid measuring cup or a bowl with a spout. Divide the custard among the ramekins, covering the berries. The mixture should come within ⅛ inch of the rim.

Carefully place the pans in the oven. Ideally, you should put them side by side on the lower rack. If they can't fit together, place one on the center rack and one on the lower one. Very carefully pour boiling water into each pan so that it comes two-thirds of the way up the sides of the ramekins.

Bake until the centers of the custards are set and an instant-read thermometer inserted in the centers registers 185°F, 30 to 40 minutes.

Carefully remove the ramekins from the water and cool on a wire rack for 30 minutes. Refrigerate uncovered until cold and set, at least 4 hours or up to 1 day.

About half an hour before you're ready to serve, sprinkle 1½ teaspoons turbinado sugar evenly on top of each custard. Use a kitchen torch to caramelize the sugar, letting it bubble and turn very dark brown. Return to the refrigerator and chill for 20 minutes, then serve immediately.

1 cup strawberries, hulled and cut in eighths

½ cup raspberries, halved

½ cup blackberries, halved

3 cups heavy cream

½ cup granulated sugar

⅛ teaspoon salt

1 vanilla bean, halved lengthwise

9 large egg yolks

12 teaspoons turbinado sugar

*Mel i Mató*

# HONEY AND GOAT CHEESE CUSTARDS

SERVES 8

Mel i mató translates to "honey and cheese" and refers to a local fresh cow's or goat's milk cheese. The dessert, originally from Catalonia, is nothing more than a round of that cheese with local honey drizzled on top. When both those products are perfect, the dessert is, too.

To capture the spirit of the unadulterated original in a more modern dessert, I turn goat cheese into panna cotta. Catalonia's mató is nearly as soft and creamy as panna cotta, so it's almost like making the cheese at home. While the custards and honey need nothing more, they do taste great with brandied peaches (page 245).

1¼ cups whole milk

1 tablespoon powdered unsweetened gelatin

3¼ cups heavy cream

½ cup tightly packed fresh mint leaves

10 ounces goat cheese, such as Capricho de Cabra

⅓ cup honey, plus more for drizzling

⅛ teaspoon salt

POUR THE MILK INTO A MEDIUM SAUCEPAN, THEN sprinkle the gelatin evenly on top. Let stand for 10 minutes at room temperature to hydrate the gelatin. Fill a large bowl with ice and water.

Bring the cream and mint to a simmer in a large saucepan over medium heat. Remove from the heat and let stand for 5 minutes. Remove and discard the mint leaves. Meanwhile, crumble the goat cheese into a large bowl.

Heat the milk and gelatin mixture over medium heat, stirring continuously to dissolve the gelatin. As soon as the gelatin dissolves, remove from the heat and stir in the honey and salt. Continue stirring while adding the warm minted cream in a steady stream. Pour the cream-milk mixture over the goat cheese and whisk until very smooth. Set over the bowl of ice and water and stir often until the mixture has thickened and an instant-read thermometer registers 50°F.

Pour the mixture through a fine-mesh sieve into a 2-quart liquid measuring cup or a bowl with a spout. Divide among eight 4-ounce ramekins. Cover tightly with plastic wrap and refrigerate until set, at least 8 hours and up to 1 day.

When ready to serve, fill a small bowl with boiling water. Hold a ramekin in the water for 5 seconds, then lift out the ramekin and wipe the outside dry. Center a serving plate over the ramekin and invert the plate and ramekin together. Slowly lift off the ramekin. The panna cotta should slide out. If it doesn't, loosen the edges by lightly tugging the edges in toward the center with damp fingers. Repeat with the remaining ramekins. Serve with the Brandied Peaches (page 245, optional) and drizzle with honey.

*Melocotones en Almíbar*

# BRANDIED PEACHES

SERVES 8 TO 12

Preserving is big in Spain. Not just now, but going back generations. The same is true in Asheville—and all over the South. Peaches are often kept in syrup and served as dessert. I like to spike them with brandy and serve them with a Catalan classic, Mel i Mató (page 242). They're also fantastic over ice cream (pages 256 to 257).

**8 large peaches**

**1 cup sugar**

**1 cup brandy**

**B**RING A LARGE SAUCEPAN OF WATER TO BOIL. Fill a large bowl with ice and water. Score the bottom of each peach with an "X." Place in the boiling water and poach, turning, for 30 to 45 seconds to release the peel from the flesh. Use a slotted spoon to transfer to the ice water. When cool enough to handle, slip the skins off the peaches. Halve the peaches and discard the pits, then cut into ½-inch-thick wedges.

Bring the sugar, brandy, and ¾ cup water to a boil in a large saucepan, stirring to dissolve the sugar. Add the peaches and simmer for 1 minute. Transfer to a heatproof container and let the peaches cool in the syrup.

The peaches can be covered tightly and refrigerated for up to 1 week.

# BAKED APRICOTS WITH SWEET YOGURT MOUSSE AND PINE OIL

### SERVES 8

I created this dessert and named it "flavors of the Mediterranean" because the combination reminds me of the time I spent at elBulli. I would drive along the Mediterranean coast every day to get to work. Along the way, I could pick super-ripe apricots from the farmers' market. Once I got to work, I often helped pick pine needles from the trees outside and watched my colleagues shuck pine nuts from their cones for a pine nut risotto dish. To tie those elements together, I whip yogurt for a creamy base.

Even if you don't live in a Mediterranean climate, chances are you're near a pine tree somewhere. I have southern pines in my backyard, but northern white pines will do, too. (The spinach makes the oil a vibrant green color.) The we're-on-a-hike woodsy aroma is intoxicating and brings out the best in sweet-tart apricots.

### BAKED APRICOTS

**8 apricots, halved and pitted**

**¼ cup honey**

### PINE OIL

**¼ cup fresh pine needles, free of any pesticides or herbicides**

**½ cup extra-virgin olive oil**

**6 baby spinach leaves, optional**

**Candied Nuts and Seeds (page 44) for serving**

### SWEET YOGURT MOUSSE

**1½ cups heavy cream**

**3 tablespoons granulated sugar**

**¾ cup plain Greek yogurt**

To make the apricots, preheat the oven to 350°F.

Place a very large sheet of foil on a half-sheet pan. Arrange the apricots on the foil, cut sides up, in a single layer. Drizzle the honey evenly on top. Bring up the sides of the foil and seal to create a packet.

Bake until the apricots are tender but still hold their shape, 20 to 30 minutes. Uncover the apricots and let cool in the foil until room temperature. The apricots with their juices can be refrigerated in an airtight container for up to 3 days. Bring to room temperature before using.

While the apricots cool, make the pine oil. Cover the pine needles with water in a small bowl. Swish to remove any dirt and debris. Repeat until the water is clear. Drain well and pat dry. Transfer to a blender and add the oil, and spinach if using, to keep the oil a bright green color. Blend on high speed until the oil is green and the pine needles are broken into tiny bits. Strain through a fine-mesh sieve. The oil can be refrigerated in an airtight container for up to 1 week. Bring to room temperature and whisk before using.

Just before serving, make the yogurt mousse. Whisk the cream and sugar in a medium bowl until soft peaks form. Whisk the yogurt in a large bowl until smooth. Fold in one-quarter of the whipped cream until well mixed, then fold in the remaining until incorporated.

Divide the pine oil among 8 serving bowls, then top with the apricot halves and yogurt mousse. Sprinkle with the candied pine nuts and serve immediately.

*Arroz con Leche*

# FLOATING ISLANDS

SERVES 8

This is my interpretation of a beloved dessert from Madrid and Asturias, arroz con leche. I make a crème anglaise with the rice and the spices normally cooked into a pudding. That creamy sauce becomes the base for floating island poached meringues. You get all the soulful comfort of rice pudding in light-as-air bites. To make this for a dinner party, do the crème anglaise days ahead, then whip and poach the meringues right before serving.

**ARROZ CON LECHE CRÈME ANGLAISE**

**1 cup long-grain white rice**

**5 cinnamon sticks, snapped in half, plus 1 for garnish**

**2½ cups heavy cream**

**2½ cups milk**

**1 lemon**

**½ cup granulated sugar**

**4 large egg yolks**

**MERINGUES**

**4 large egg whites**

**¼ teaspoon cream of tartar**

**½ cup superfine sugar**

**T**O MAKE THE CRÈME ANGLAISE, COMBINE THE rice and cinnamon sticks in a large saucepan and toast over medium heat, stirring occasionally, until fragrant and a shade darker, about 15 minutes. Add the cream and milk. Using a vegetable peeler, remove strips of lemon peel from half the lemon and add to the saucepan. Reduce the heat to medium-low and heat, vigorously stirring often to prevent sticking, until an instant-read thermometer registers 185°F. The mixture will be hot to the touch; do not heat too quickly or let the temperature exceed 185°F. Remove from the heat and let stand, uncovered, for 30 minutes, stirring every 10 minutes.

Strain the mixture through a medium-mesh sieve into a 1-quart liquid measuring cup, pressing on the solids to extract as much liquid as possible. Discard the solids. You should have 4 cups liquid. If not, add equal parts milk and cream to bring the volume up to 4 cups. Return to the saucepan and bring to a bare simmer over medium-low heat.

While the liquid heats, whisk the granulated sugar and egg yolks in a large bowl. Continue whisking while adding the hot liquid in a slow, steady stream. Return to the saucepan and heat over medium-low heat, stirring continuously, until the mixture is just thick enough to coat the spatula and an instant-read thermometer registers 185°F. Do not heat the mixture past this temperature or it will curdle. Transfer to a bowl and set in a larger bowl of ice and water to cool. Stir occasionally until cold. When cold, divide among 8 serving bowls. The chilled crème anglaise can be refrigerated in an airtight container for up to 3 days.

Meanwhile, make the meringues. Using the whisk attachment of an electric mixer, beat the egg whites and cream of tartar in a large bowl until foamy. While whisking, add the superfine sugar in a steady stream. Beat until the whites are glossy and hold soft peaks.

Fill a large, deep skillet with water to a depth of 1½ inches. Bring to a simmer over high heat, then reduce the heat to medium-low to maintain a bare simmer. Using a large spoon, dollop half of the meringue mixture in 4 mounds into the simmering water. The water should not boil. If it's bubbling too hard, lower the heat. Cook until just set on the bottom, about 2 minutes. Gently flip the meringues and cook for 2 minutes longer. Use a slotted spoon to transfer to half of the serving dishes with crème anglaise. Repeat with the remaining meringue mixture. Zest the cinnamon stick and remaining lemon half all over the tops and serve immediately.

**ARROZ CON LECHE ICE CREAM:** Make only the Arroz con Leche Crème Anglaise and refrigerate overnight. Churn in an ice cream maker according to the manufacturer's instructions. Serve immediately or freeze in airtight containers until firm.

*Sabayón de Chocolate*

# CHOCOLATE-BRANDY SABAYON

SERVES 6 TO 8

At Cúrate, we serve a warm chocolate mousse made by holding ganache and egg whites in an immersion circulator, then siphoning the hot blend into dishes. I wanted to do a version for the home kitchen and it turns out chocolate sabayon is the answer. It's ironic. Home cooks can't do what we do at the restaurant because they lack the equipment, and we can't make sabayon during our high-volume restaurant service for lack of manpower and space. But you end up with the same dessert either way.

Even though chocolate's always delicious on its own, it's even better when whipped with brandy. The final topping of tart raspberries with salt and olive oil transforms the dish into a restaurant-worthy dessert.

6 large egg yolks

½ cup sugar

¼ cup brandy

2 tablespoons unsweetened cocoa powder

2 ounces bittersweet chocolate, preferably 60% cacao, finely chopped

Raspberries, for serving

Maldon sea salt, for serving

Extra-virgin olive oil, for serving

WHISK THE EGG YOLKS AND SUGAR IN A MEdium heatproof bowl until pale yellow. Whisk in the brandy, cocoa powder, and ½ cup water until smooth.

Set the bowl over a saucepan of simmering water and whisk continuously until thick and an instant-read thermometer registers 165°F, about 12 minutes. Remove from the heat and whisk in the chocolate until smooth.

Divide among serving dishes and top with raspberries. Sprinkle with salt, drizzle with oil, and serve immediately.

*Turrón de Alicante*

# FROZEN MERINGUE WITH CANDIED MARCONA ALMONDS AND GRAND MARNIER

MAKES ONE 9- BY 5-INCH LOAF;
SERVES 8 TO 12

For Christmas, turrón de Alicante, an almond honey nougat, is served all over Spain. Cúrate's version isn't a candy, but uses the same ingredients to make a soft frozen dessert. It has the chill and mallowy softness of a semifreddo and the crunchy sweet almonds reminiscent of traditional turrón. Our meringue is actually easier to execute than the candy, and, in my opinion, more pleasurable to eat because it doesn't get stuck in your teeth.

**CANDIED MARCONA ALMONDS**

½ cup granulated sugar

3 tablespoons unsalted butter

1 tablespoon light corn syrup

¼ teaspoon kosher salt

¼ teaspoon baking soda

1 cup roasted salted Marcona almonds

**SEMIFREDDO**

½ cup granulated sugar

1 tablespoon light corn syrup

2 large egg whites, room temperature

⅛ teaspoon kosher salt

1⅓ cups heavy cream

1 tablespoon plus 1 teaspoon Grand Marnier

Zest of 1 small orange

TO MAKE THE CANDIED ALMONDS, LINE A HALF-sheet pan with a nonstick baking mat or well-greased foil. Bring the sugar, butter, corn syrup, and 3 tablespoons water to a boil in a large saucepan over medium heat. Cook, stirring occasionally, until the sugar begins to caramelize and turns a light golden brown, about 4 minutes. Stir in the salt, baking soda, and almonds until the almonds are evenly coated. Cook until the caramel is a dark shade of amber, about 2 minutes. Remove from heat and immediately pour onto the prepared pan. Using a heatproof silicone spatula or metal offset spatula, carefully and quickly spread in an even layer. Cool completely on the pan on a wire rack, then coarsely chop.

Meanwhile, make the meringue. Line a 9- by 5-inch loaf pan with plastic wrap with overhang on all four sides. Use 2 crisscrossing sheets of plastic wrap if needed.

Bring the sugar, corn syrup, and 3 tablespoons water to a boil in a small saucepan over medium heat. Cook, stirring, until the sugar dissolves, then simmer without stirring until a candy thermometer registers 248°F. While the sugar mixture simmers, whip the egg whites with the whisk attachment of an electric mixer on medium-low speed until foamy. Add the salt, raise the speed to medium, and whip until soft peaks form. Reduce the speed to low. With the machine running, slowly and carefully pour the hot sugar syrup into the bowl in a steady stream. Pour along the side of the bowl so that the whisk doesn't flick burning hot beads of sugar out of the bowl. Raise the speed to high and whisk until the mixture stops steaming, about 3 minutes. Reserve the meringue.

Whisk the cream in a clean, cold large bowl with a clean whisk attachment or electric mixer until soft peaks form. Fold in the Grand Marnier and orange zest until incorporated, then fold in the meringue and candied Marcona almonds just until no streaks of egg whites remain. Do not overmix or let the mixture deflate.

Carefully scrape the meringue into the prepared pan. Use an offset spatula to create swirls and peaks on top.

Freeze until firmer, at least overnight and up to 3 days. The meringue won't—and shouldn't—freeze into a hard solid.

To serve, lift the meringue out of the pan using the plastic overhang. Unwrap and cut into slices.

(Clockwise, from top)
Raspberry Lavender Sorbet,
Roasted Strawberry–
Watermelon Cava Sorbet,
Salted Rosemary Ice Cream,
Lemon and Thyme Ice Cream

*Sorbete de Sandía y Fresa con Cava*

# ROASTED STRAWBERRY-WATERMELON CAVA SORBET

**MAKES 5 CUPS**

For me, this is summertime in a dessert. It's an icier sorbet that's refreshing and not too sweet. Roasting the strawberries first intensify their flavor; be sure to scrape up all of the juices and syrup from the roasting pan, too. To complement the sweetness of those berries and fresh watermelon, use a brut or dry cava. A scoop of this sorbet is the ideal way to end a light summer meal, but it can also work as a palate cleanser between heavier dishes, like grilled meats.

**8 ounces strawberries, hulled**

**1 tablespoon blended oil**

**¾ cup plus 2 tablespoons granulated sugar, divided**

**4 cups watermelon chunks**

**2 tablespoons fresh lemon juice**

**1 cup brut cava**

**P**REHEAT THE OVEN TO 375°F. TOSS THE STRAW-berries, oil, and 2 tablespoons sugar on a half-sheet pan. Arrange the strawberries in a single layer, hulled side down. Roast for 10 minutes, rotate the pan, and roast for 10 minutes more. Cool completely on the pan on a wire rack.

Bring the remaining ¾ cup sugar and ¾ cup water to a boil in a small saucepan, stirring to dissolve the sugar. Remove the simple syrup from the heat and cool completely.

Scrape the strawberries with all their pan juices into a blender and add the watermelon and simple syrup. Puree until very smooth. Strain through a fine-mesh sieve into an airtight container, and whisk in the lemon juice and cava. Cover and refrigerate until very cold, at least 8 hours and up to overnight.

Churn the chilled mixture in an ice cream maker according to the manufacturer's instructions. Serve immediately or freeze in an airtight container for up to 1 week.

# RASPBERRY LAVENDER SORBET

⟶⟵

MAKES 5 CUPS

Lavender grows all over Spain. When used in its fresh form, its floral fragrance stays subtle. That hint of lavender perfumes this sweet-tart raspberry sorbet, elevating its otherwise straightforward flavors into an elegant dessert complex enough to eat on its own.

| | |
|---|---|
| ¾ cup granulated sugar | 1½ pounds frozen raspberries |
| 1 cup packed fresh lavender sprigs, tied with twine into a bundle | 2 tablespoons vodka |

**B**RING THE SUGAR, LAVENDER, AND 1 CUP WATER to a boil in a large saucepan, stirring to dissolve the sugar. Stir in the raspberries and bring to a simmer. Remove from the heat, cover, and let stand for 30 minutes.

Discard the lavender. Transfer the raspberry mixture to a blender and puree on high speed, scraping the bowl occasionally, until very smooth, at least 1 minute. Add the vodka and blend until fully incorporated.

Pass the mixture through a fine-mesh sieve, pressing on the solids to extract as much liquid as possible. Refrigerate in an airtight container until very cold, at least 8 hours and up to overnight.

Churn the chilled mixture in an ice cream maker according to the manufacturer's instructions. Serve immediately or freeze in an airtight container for up to 1 week.

# SALTED ROSEMARY ICE CREAM

⟶⟵

MAKES 1 QUART

Rosemary is one of my favorite herbs, so I don't restrict my use of it to savory dishes. That being said, I decided to add a pinch of salt to this ice cream to accentuate rosemary's piney fragrance. This dessert is especially delicious served with bits of dark chocolate and drizzled with olive oil.

| | |
|---|---|
| 1½ cups whole milk | 6 large egg yolks |
| 1½ cups heavy cream | ¾ cup granulated sugar |
| 1 cup packed rosemary sprigs | 1 teaspoon kosher salt |

**B**RING THE MILK, CREAM, AND ROSEMARY TO A boil in a medium saucepan. Remove from the heat and let stand for 10 minutes. Strain through a fine-mesh sieve.

Meanwhile, whisk the egg yolks and sugar in a medium saucepan until smooth. Whisk in the strained hot cream in a slow, steady stream. Set over medium-low heat and cook, stirring continuously, until thickened slightly and an instant-read thermometer registers 175°F. Avoid overcooking the mixture so that it doesn't curdle. Strain through a fine-mesh sieve into another bowl and stir in the salt. Set the bowl in a larger bowl of ice and water to quickly cool to room temperature. Transfer to an airtight container and refrigerate for at least 8 hours and up to overnight.

Churn the chilled mixture in an ice cream maker according to the manufacturer's instructions. Serve immediately or freeze in an airtight container for up to 1 week.

# LEMON AND THYME ICE CREAM

## MAKES 1 QUART

A little cup of lemon sorbet is a classic dessert in Spain. I figured I'd like it even more if transformed into an ice cream. I love ice cream, particularly a lemon one that melds acidity and richness. In order to incorporate a lot of lemon flavor without curdling the milk or cream, we make a curd with extra eggs. That addition stabilizes the ice cream base and results in an intensely creamy final texture. You will notice after the base sets that it is almost thick. Don't worry, that's what you're looking for. A stand-alone scoop is great for a casual dessert, but scatter a few fresh blackberries on top to end a fancier meal.

¾ cup whole milk

1 cup heavy cream

1½ cups packed thyme sprigs

1½ cups granulated sugar

Zest of 1 lemon

¾ cup fresh lemon juice

3 large egg yolks

6 large eggs

Blackberries, for garnish (optional)

**B**RING THE MILK, CREAM, AND THYME TO A BOIL in a medium saucepan. Remove from the heat and let stand for 15 minutes. Strain through a fine-mesh sieve.

Meanwhile, whisk the sugar, lemon zest and juice, egg yolks, and whole eggs in a medium bowl. Set over a saucepan of simmering water and heat, stirring continuously, until thickened and an instant-read thermometer registers 160°F, about 8 minutes. Whisk in the strained cream mixture, then strain through a fine-mesh sieve into another bowl. Set the bowl in a larger bowl of ice and water to quickly cool to room temperature. Transfer to an airtight container and refrigerate for at least 8 hours and up to overnight.

Churn the chilled mixture in an ice cream maker according to the manufacturer's instructions. Serve immediately, with blackberries if you'd like, or freeze in an airtight container for up to 1 week.

# DRINKS

# SPANISH WINES

AT CÚRATE, FÉLIX PUT TOGETHER A WINE LIST THAT features only Spanish vineyards. We don't source from any other country because there's such a diversity of styles from different regions, much like the cuisine. Plus, Spanish wines are a relative bargain. The quality you get for the price you pay is pretty fantastic. And as you move up in quality and price you get an even better value.

Spanish wines are produced in different regions all over the country, from the popular Rioja, Ribera del Duero, Galicia, and Catalonia to lesser-known wine producers like the Canary Islands, Madrid, and Jerez. At Cúrate, we strive to showcase the best of all the different regions. In fact, in Spain it would be difficult to find the variety we offer. Most restaurants and bars serve only the wines of their own regions. It makes sense because their dishes match best with their wines. They come from the same soil, after all. Since I like to cook foods from all over the country, I like to serve them with wines that match. But the truth is that there isn't one right wine for each dish.

Throughout the book, you will see recommended pairings for certain dishes, but they're meant to be suggestions, not rules. Because Spanish wineries are getting better and better at selling what's ready to drink (not just bottles to hold), you can try a bunch of different Spanish wines and see what you like . . . and then keep trying more and more. You won't have to spend a lot in the process and you'll discover a whole new world of wine.

# SANGRÍAS

We do a unique sangría at Cúrate. In Spain,
sangría is usually mixed with fruit and ice
early and doled out by the glass all day long.
At Cúrate, we make sangría the way we mix
cocktails: right before serving so that it tastes
extra fresh. This technique still works well
for entertaining because all the components
can—and should—be chilled far ahead of
time. The final mixing takes seconds. One
modern Spanish tradition we've upheld is
the use of Sprite. I've tried homemade syrups
and sodas, but they don't replicate the same
lemon-lime fizz found in Spanish sangrías.

Both of the refreshing drinks here are
easy to put together and form a blank canvas
for the best herbs and fruit of the season.
Nearly any combination of fruit and herbs
works well. Some of my favorites are peaches
and blackberries, watermelon, and strawberries, and any mix of citrus. Classic herbs
like mint taste great, as do aromatics such as
lemon verbena.

# CAVA SANGRÍA

SERVES 6 TO 8

3 tablespoons cognac

3 tablespoons gin

3 tablespoons Cointreau

3 tablespoons Simple Syrup (page 269)

1 cup cut-up seasonal fruit, such as watermelon and berries

1 lime wheel

1 strip orange zest, removed with a vegetable peeler

1 750-ml bottle cava, chilled until very cold

STIR THE COGNAC, GIN, COINTREAU, SIMPLE syrup, fruit, lime wheel, and orange zest in a pitcher. Refrigerate until very cold, at least 1 hour and up to 4 hours.

When ready to serve, stir in the cava. Divide among glasses and serve immediately.

# RED SANGRÍA

SERVES 6 TO 8

### CITRUS SPICE SYRUP

¾ cup fresh orange juice, plus zest of ½ orange, removed with a vegetable peeler

¼ cup fresh lemon juice, plus zest of ½ lemon, removed with a vegetable peeler

3 tablespoons sugar

5 juniper berries

5 black peppercorns

1 cinnamon stick

1 mint sprig

1 fresh or dried bay leaf

### SANGRÍA

6 tablespoons cognac

1 orange wheel

1 lemon wheel

2 cups cut-up fresh seasonal fruit, such as peaches and citrus

½ cup Sprite, chilled until very cold

1 750-ml bottle dry red wine, preferably Garnacha, or any fruit-forward affordable red wine, chilled until very cold

TO MAKE THE SYRUP, BRING EVERYTHING TO A simmer with 3 tablespoons water. Cover, remove from the heat, and let stand for 30 minutes. Strain through a fine-mesh sieve into an airtight container. Refrigerate until cold, at least 4 hours and up to 1 week.

To make the sangría, fill a pitcher with ice, then add the cognac, orange wheel, lemon wheel, fruit, and citrus spice syrup. Pour in the Sprite and wine and stir to combine. Serve immediately over ice.

# THE PERFECT GIN AND TONIC

The gin and tonic is the cocktail of Spain. Spaniards take the G&T very seriously. They're always debating which tonic pairs best with which types of gin and how to garnish the drink. I'm not so fussy as to insist that you garnish with cucumber if you're pouring Hendricks. I think you should use whichever gin you enjoy drinking most. (Félix and I like Plymouth or Millers.) As for the tonic, I suggest you look for Fever Tree, which has just the right balance of bitter and sweet. Once you gather your ingredients—ice, lemon, gin, and tonic—the real work begins. A good gin and tonic is all about execution. Here's how Félix does it.

**1.** Chill the glass by filling it to the brim with ice and letting it sit until cold. We like to use a large balloon-shaped glass, such as a brandy glass.

**2.** Remove a 6-inch strip of lemon peel with a sharp paring knife or vegetable peeler, curving around the fruit as needed to get it in a single strip. If there's any white pith left on the back of the peel, shave it off with the knife.

**3.** Toss out the ice in the glass.

**4.** Squeeze the lemon peel over the glass so that the citrus oils spray into the glass, then run the peel around the rim.

**5.** Fill the glass halfway with ice, preferably with 4 or 5 large cocktail ice cubes. Add the gin, then pour in chilled tonic over a spoon, so that it doesn't foam up. (We use 1½ ounces gin to 4 ounces tonic, then adjust to taste.) Stir once or twice, but don't over-stir or you'll lose the bubbles and the aromatics.

**6.** Drop the lemon peel in the glass and enjoy!

THE **PERFECT GIN** AND **TONIC**

# COCKTAILS

Mixology may be making inroads in Spain, but it's still relatively new. Cocktails play a big role at Cúrate though because Félix is passionate about them, as are our diners. When he creates cocktails, he takes inspiration from Spanish produce, liqueurs, wines, and cooking techniques. The only traditional cocktail on our menu—and here—is the rebujito, which hails from the south as a refresher for hot days. The others are our own creations, but taste like they're deeply rooted in the culture. They're the perfect aperitifs for any Spanish meal.

Eclipse de Luna

## REBUJITO

MUDDLE A MINT SPRIG IN THE BOTTOM OF A LARGE rocks glass. Fill with ice and add 2 ounces Manzanilla sherry, preferably La Cigarerra. Top off with 6 ounces chilled Fever Tree Bitter Lemon soda and stir.

## SIDRA CAR

SHAKE 1½ OUNCES GRAND MARNIER, ½ OUNCE fresh lemon juice, and ¼ ounce Simple Syrup (recipe follows) over ice. Strain into a martini glass, then top off with 2 ounces chilled Poma Áurea or other Spanish sparkling cider. Top with a very thin apple round and freshly grated lime zest.

## SPANISH MARTINI

SQUEEZE A STRIP OF ORANGE PEEL (REMOVED FROM an orange with a vegetable peeler) over a martini glass to release the citrus oil, then drop the peel into the glass. Shake 1½ ounces vodka, 1 ounce Licor 43, ½ ounce Cointreau, and ½ ounce fresh lemon juice over ice. Strain into the glass.

## ECLIPSE DE LUNA

STIR 1 OUNCE MOONSHINE OR OTHER WHITE WHISKEY and ½ ounce Oloroso sherry in a large rocks glass. Fill with ice and top off with 4 ounces ginger ale, preferably Fever Tree. Stir and garnish with an orange round and cinnamon stick.

## JEREZ SOUR

SHAKE 1 OUNCE SPANISH BRANDY, PREFERABLY Gran Duque d'Alba, 1 ounce Oloroso sherry, 1 ounce fresh lemon juice, ½ ounce Simple Syrup (recipe follows) a dash of orange bitters, and 1 teaspoon juice from a jar of Luxardo maraschino cherries with ice. Strain into a large rocks glass filled with ice. Top off with 1½ ounces soda water and garnish with a cherry from the jar.

## SIMPLE SYRUP

BRING ½ CUP GRANULATED SUGAR AND ½ CUP water to a boil in a small saucepan, stirring to dissolve the sugar. Cool completely. The syrup can be refrigerated in an airtight container for up to 1 week. Makes ¾ cup (6 ounces).

Rebujito        Sidra Car        Spanish Martini        Jerez Sour

# BEER

SPAIN'S A HOT COUNTRY, SO EVERYONE'S ALWAYS looking for something cool to drink. Beer's an obvious choice, but you can't very well drink beer all day. That's why the panaché is so popular. It's more or less 50/50 beer and lemon soda. At Cúrate, we combine a lager with Fever Tree's Bitter Lemon Soda. If we're serving panaché to a big party, we recommend trying the porrón. It's like a watering can to quench your thirst. It's usually used for wine, but because it takes some skill to pour that arc of alcohol into your mouth from a distance, we swapped clothes-staining red wine for light-colored panaché. Our guests love passing the porrón around the table and taking shots at drinking. It's a fun party game you can try at home. You can buy a nice porrón online or in specialty stores.

For straight-up beer, we don't head across the Atlantic for our bar selection. In Spain, you get whatever regional lager is on draft. (There's usually only one.) In that spirit, we get our beer from Asheville, which produces so many different varieties of craft brews. From downtown extending out to West Asheville, breweries seem to pop up overnight. There are often two or more on a single block, converted from old manufacturing warehouses or built in new developments. The variety is as impressive as the quality. A lot of Spain's big flavors, particularly the savory ones, taste even better with a cold glass of beer.

# ROM CREMAT

**SERVES 4 TO 6**

1 750-ml bottle gold rum, such as Bacardi

¼ cup granulated sugar

3 tablespoons coffee beans

1 lemon, zest removed with a vegetable peeler

1 cinnamon stick

Rom cremat comes from the fishermen villages of the Costa Brava. It started as a warming drink for fishermen deep at sea, then made its way on to land, where it became a staple of village celebrations. At the festivities that commemorate the villages, rom cremat burns in pots throughout the old streets while everyone dances and sings habaneras. The tradition extends only as far as the civil war, when many Spaniards immigrated to Cuba and developed a taste for rum and the swaying songs of the island. When they returned, they brought this drink with them. The dramatic flames not only convey good times but also burn off much of the alcohol and distill the rum's full-bodied flavor. A bottle of rum for 4 to 6 people may sound like a lot, but most of it disappears before it's divvied up.

If the idea of setting a pot of liquor on fire sounds a little dangerous, it's because it is. Be sure to follow the instructions here and keep in mind that you're making this drink at your own risk.

STIR THE RUM, SUGAR, COFFEE BEANS, LEMON zest, and cinnamon stick in a large Dutch oven. Set on the grate of an outdoor kettle grill without any charcoal or anything else that can ignite. Make sure the grill is far from any trees, shrubs, or other flammable objects. With a long lighter, ignite the rum. Let the flame burn for 10 minutes, then extinguish by putting on the lid to snuff out the fire.

After the flame completely dies out, immediately divide among small cups, leaving the coffee beans, zest, and cinnamon behind. Serve hot.

*Horchata*

# CHUFA NUT MILK

MAKES ABOUT 3½ CUPS

Most of the horchata in the U.S. has its origins in Latin America, where it's made with rice or seeds. In Valencia, it starts with chufa nuts, also known as tiger nuts, which are actually tiny, starchy dried tubers related to water chestnuts. They have a nutty sweetness similar to almonds and the process of turning them into a drink actually resembles that of making almond milk. Chufa nuts are easy to find online and in health food stores and, increasingly, everywhere since they're being touted as the next super food. I don't know about all that, but I do know they're delicious.

Traditionally, the milk is sweetened, but it tastes good even without sugar. I've started with a minimal amount of simple syrup; you can add more if you'd like. In the summer, the chilled drink is extremely refreshing. In the winter, it's wonderful as a stand in for eggnog. It shares a creamy richness, but is much lighter.

**2 cups chufa nuts (tiger nuts)**

**⅓ cup Simple Syrup (page 269) plus more to taste**

COVER THE CHUFA NUTS WITH COLD WATER BY 2 inches in an airtight container. Refrigerate overnight.

Strain through a fine-mesh sieve into a 1-quart liquid measuring cup; reserve the nuts. Add water, if needed, for 4 cups total liquid. Pour the liquid into a blender and add the nuts. Puree on high speed until very, very smooth.

Pour the mixture through a fine-mesh sieve in batches, pressing on the solids to extract as much liquid as possible. Discard the solids. Pour the mixture through the sieve two more times, but don't press on any remaining solids. Stir in the simple syrup and add more to taste if you'd like.

Serve immediately over ice or refrigerate in an airtight container until very cold.

The horchata can be refrigerated in an airtight container for up to 1 week. Shake or stir before serving.

# HORCHATA COCKTAIL

1 strip orange peel (removed from an orange with a vegetable peeler), plus orange zest for garnish

2½ ounces Horchata (opposite)

1 ounce Spanish brandy, preferably Gran Duque d'Alba

½ ounce Grand Marnier

Cinnamon stick, for garnish

**S**QUEEZE THE ORANGE PEEL OVER A LARGE martini glass, rub the rim with the peel, then drop the peel into the glass. Shake the Horchata, brandy, and Grand Marnier with ice. Strain and pour into the glass. Grate a cinnamon stick and a little orange zest over the drink. Serve immediately.

*Limonada de Estragón y Romero*

# TARRAGON AND ROSEMARY LEMONADE

꩜

**MAKES ABOUT 4½ CUPS**

My chefs sometimes joke that I throw tarragon and lemon into everything. I love that flavor combination (it pops up throughout this book) and this virgin drink highlights how tarragon and lemon taste great together. The addition of the herbaceous rosemary really balances out the combination and makes this nonalcoholic drink as special as any cocktail.

**1 cup granulated sugar**

**2 rosemary sprigs, plus more for garnish**

**4 tarragon sprigs, plus more for garnish**

**1½ cups cold fresh lemon juice**

BRING THE SUGAR AND 1 CUP WATER TO A BOIL IN a small saucepan, stirring to dissolve the sugar. Add the rosemary and tarragon and cover. Remove from the heat and let stand for 30 minutes. Remove the herbs and transfer the syrup to a pitcher.

Stir in the lemon juice and 1½ cups ice-cold water. The lemonade can be refrigerated for up to 3 days. When ready to serve, pour over ice and garnish with rosemary and tarragon.

# ACKNOWLEDGMENTS

## KATIE BUTTON

This book wouldn't have come to fruition if our editor, Will Schwalbe, hadn't come in to eat at Cúrate. I owe it to Will for planting the idea of a cookbook in my head. I am forever grateful to our publisher, Bob Miller, for wholeheartedly agreeing with Will and taking on this project. I'm also grateful to Kara Rota for her wonderful insight and direction throughout the process and to Bryn Clark, Kimberly Escobar, Molly Fonseca, and Marlena Bittner. Thanks to Shubhani Sarkar for designing all of the pages so beautifully. And thank you to the entire staff at Flatiron Books for being such a wonderful and supportive company and for guiding me through my first book!

Lisa Abend connected me to David Black, our literary agent. I can't thank her enough for directing us to someone so dedicated to making this book, my restaurants, and me a success. Thank you David for always being there, no matter what hour of the day, whenever I needed advice; I know that this is the beginning of a long friendship.

Genevieve Ko, our writer, took our mishmash of ideas and magically made them flow eloquently on the pages. Genevieve is both a wonderful writer and a fantastic, precise recipe tester. She was a pleasure to work with on this project.

While I was busy recipe testing for this book, my staff at both of my restaurants, Cúrate and Nightbell, ran things seamlessly without me. The amount that we have accomplished in the past five years has been incredible. I can't wait to see what the next five will bring.

Allegra Grant made the days of recipe testing in my home fly by with her attention to detail and passion for cooking. Meanwhile, Ana Myers, our nanny, cared for our most precious package, our daughter Gisela, during the cookbook process.

A special thank-you goes out to Frank Muller and Carmen Vaquera for working long, hard days to prepare all of the dishes for the photo shoot. And thanks to our manager Nathan Lanham for ensuring Cúrate operated smoothly and for guest bartending at the shoot. I still can't believe how much we accomplished in that short amount of time. Evan Sung, our photographer, made all of our dishes come to life. Without his agreement to work on this project with us, the final product would never have been the same. Kira Corbin, the prop stylist, made the food more beautiful than we ever could have imagined. Ron Basil and AVL Luxury Vacation Rentals allowed us to use one of their homes. The bear and lynxes that came to visit us during the photo shoot provided us with a little excitement and a lot of comic relief.

Thank you to all of the farmers and producers in Asheville and in Spain, who have dedicated their lives to creating products that we use in our restaurants and that inspired the dishes for this cookbook. We're also grateful to the Asheville artisans who supplied the surfaces we shot on for this book's photography. A big thank you to Antique Hardwood & Beams, Dynamic Metalwork, and Mountain Marble.

I'm grateful to Liz Pierson and Lissie Chappell of Becca PR for spreading the news about this book. Thank you to my mentors, José Andrés, Ferran Adrià, and Albert Adrià, for giving me the opportunity to work for you. José, you came to the opening of Cúrate and provided support when we needed it most, and since then you have continued to give me opportunities in this career. Ferran and Albert, I wouldn't be the chef I am today had I not stepped foot in elBulli. You and your team taught me professionalism, organization, and the belief that I can achieve as much as I want to in this life and as a chef. I also want to thank Johnny Iuzzini for inviting me into his kitchen for my first professional cooking position.

My parents, Liz and Ted Button, have believed in me and have been there every step of the way, as family and as business partners. My mother, Liz, inspired me to become a chef by cooking with me when I was little and by pursuing and growing her own professional culinary career. My father, Ted, has always been there, supporting every decision I make. He took the biggest plunge when he decided to support this business venture together. It is an honor and a privilege to work beside my parents, getting to know them better than I ever would have been able to otherwise.

My brother, Shane Liddell, handles the branding and Web presence for both of our restaurants and for this book. Thanks for partnering with us over the years.

In addition to my own mother's impact, I am fortunate to have been influenced by many generations of amazing female cooks. My grandmother, Ann, and her mother created the backdrop of food culture that became my reference for delicious home-cooked meals. And my mother-in-law, Pepa, and her family introduced me to the unique traditions of Spanish cuisine. You will see throughout which cookbook recipes were influenced by Pepa's cooking.

I am sincerely grateful to my husband Félix. Without him, none of this would be possible. He is strong in every way that I am weak. He introduced me to the amazing culture in Spain, which I am proud to be a part of as a chef and as his wife. Every decision, every ingredient, every preparation, every dish was made in collaboration with him.

I want to dedicate this book to our greatest joint achievement: our daughter Gisela Meana. She was in the womb during the planning process for the cookbook and then was welcomed into the world in the midst of the recipe testing, photo shoot, and culmination of the project. I am a better person and a better chef because of her.

### GENEVIEVE KO

Thank you to Katie for so graciously welcoming me into her home, her restaurants, and her life. I'm also grateful to Félix for his warm hospitality and insight into Spanish food and life. Gisela is lucky to have two such talented and kind parents, and I'm lucky to have enjoyed her company during our cookbook sessions. Liz Button, Ted Button, Carmen Vaquera, Allegra Grant, Jacob Nygaard, and the whole Heirloom Hospitality Group helped with this book in so many ways. Evan Sung and his team complemented the recipes and stories with stunning photographs. Will Schwalbe, Kara Rota, and Bryn Clark made this book even better with their smart and thoughtful editing. Many thanks to George Mendes for introducing me to Katie, and to my agent Leslie Stoker for connecting us through David Black.

A big thanks to my family for your constant support and love.

# INDEX